I0724866

Lily POETRY REVIEW

ISSUE 12

GUEST EDITORS

Heather Treseler and Anthony Walton

EDITOR-IN-CHIEF
Eileen Cleary

ASSISTANT EDITOR
Elizabeth Mercurio

ASSOCIATE EDITOR
Christine Jones

ART EDITOR
Lisa Sullivan

BOOK REVIEW EDITOR
Amanda Shaw

VISPO EDITOR
Suzanne Mercury

WEB EDITOR
Rebecca Connors

MEDIA AND EVENTS
Frances Donovan

READERS
Susan Kay Anderson, Jules Jacob,
K. T. Landon, Michelle Lynch, Gloria Monaghan,
Catherine Morocco, Tzynya Pinchback, Sarah Dickenson Snyder,
Mark Walsh, Anastasia Vassos

DESIGN
Martha McCollough

COVER ART, ISSUE 12
Ann-Marie Brown: *Desi in Her Mother's Dress*

Letter from the Editors

In "The Poet & the City," W. H. Auden asserts that "The
characteristic style of 'Modern' poetry is an intimate tone
of voice, the speech of one person addressing one person…
whenever a poet raises his voice he sounds phony. And its
characteristic hero is…the [person] in any walk of life who,
despite the impersonal pressures of modern society, manages
to acquire and preserve a face of his own."

Editing this special edition of *Lily Poetry Review*, we cast a wide
net, soliciting work from poets throughout the United States
and from Ireland and the Ukraine, and we spent several months
reading a great store of poems, searching for that "intimate
tone" that Auden championed and a sense of the poet's doughty
determination to "preserve a face"—an existential challenge
that has arguably become more difficult as technocracy and
neoliberalism work to reduce our human voices and faces to the
demands of labor, data, and surveillance capitalism.

But what is poetry but language, approaching song, which
has incalculable value, a worth that escapes mechanisms of
economic measure? This is the personal and private virtue
that Auden hints at when he writes, in that same essay, that
whenever "a stranger in the train asks me my occupation,
I never answer 'writer.'" Instead, Auden quips, he tells his
fellow passenger that he is a "medieval historian," which
tends to punctuate the conversation.

Here, we need not disguise identities: these are poems and poets
sustaining to virtually all who encounter them—including that
proverbial stranger on a train. In gathering this cohort of talent,
we pay tribute to the late David Ferry, known and admired by
many of us as a poet, translator, and consummately kind and
gallant literary citizen, and to Eileen Cleary, Editor in Chief

of *Lily Poetry Review* and Lily Poetry Review Books, another extraordinary literary citizen who has worked tirelessly to bring the authentic voices and individual faces of poets and their poems into ever more visible circulation.

It has been a pleasure to assemble this volume, and we hope that it will help bring the work of *Lily Poetry Review*—its journal and press—into wider purview and esteem.

— Heather Treseler and Anthony Walton

DAVID FERRY
1924-2023
Poet, Translator,
Scholar.
Strangers,
Gilgamesh,
Odes of Horace,
Bewilderment,
among others
—P. Urkowitz 2024
after a photograph
by Stephen Ferry

CONTENTS

Prose

MARTHA COLLINS

If I Lived

If I lived in a certain country,
near a certain border, I would not
          live there anymore.

And if I lived across that border,
I would not live where I once lived,
          I might not live

at all, my friends might not,
my house most likely would not
          be there anymore.

And if it was, I would not have
enough to eat and drink,
          I would not have

what all must have to live in this
world that someday might not
          be here anymore.

Heat

he would turn it up and
    she would turn it down and

he would turn it up and
    she would turn it down she

thought if it were just she
    thought if he would just she

wouldn't then he died she
    wouldn't have to would then

she would turn it down and
    she would turn it up and

she would turn it down and
    turn it up and down

DYLAN RICHMOND

Thirteen Ways of Looking at a Blackboy

I
Among fifty snowed in stars,
The only moving thing
Was the heart of the blackboy.

II
To be of double consciousnesses,
Like a blackboy,
In which there can be many boys, but both black.

III
The blackboy's wail in autumn winds.
It was drowned out by white noise.

IV
A man and a woman
Are one.
A man and a woman and a blackboy
Are two and three fifths.

V
I do not know which to prefer,
The joke of inflictions
Or the joke of innuendoes,
The bullet whistling
Or just after.

VI
Icicles barred the long window
With barbaric glass.
The shadow of the blackboy
you found distorted there.
The mood
Traced in the shadow
A cause you choose not to decipher.

VII

People of Haddam,
Why do you imagine golden birds?
Do you not see how the blackboy
Is tasting himself
In the mouth of the sun?

VIII

You say you know accents,
And lucid, inescapable rhythms;
But I know, too,
That the blackboy is involved
In what you do not, cannot know.

IX

When the blackboy swam out of sight,
It marked the stretch
Of one of many oceans.

X

At the thought of blackboys
Dancing in a blue light,
The gods of you and me
Would cry out sharply.

XI

You rode through Connecticut
In a glass train.
Once, a fear pierced you,
In that you mistook
Your own gloves
For the hands of blackboys.

XII

The river is moving.
The blackboy, mourning, must be.

XIII

He was mourning all night.
It was sunrise
And the sun was going to keep rising.
The blackboy rose, too,
With his black-limbs.

JEFFERSON NAVICKY

The Houses of Gloversville

When he was a young man, my father-in-law heard of a job saving
abandoned houses in Gloversville, NY, one-time glove-making capital
of the country. It was pretty good money and he needed money and
he could do the work, so he signed on. Some of the houses had been
gutted by fire, others by flood, others still by neglect. He could feel
their loneliness leaking out like air through a drafty wooden floor.
He tried to reassure the houses that they would be alright, he was
there to help, he would take care of them, bring them back to life. It
was the same voice he used with his dog, who cried at all manner of
invisible presences. And like his dog, the houses began to relax. They
took comfort and gave treasure—a five-dollar bill under a section of
old carpet, hand-wrought nails that he tucked in his pocket, a cracked
and curling photograph of a sad-eyed young sailor tacked on the
underside of a stair tread. Inside the walls of one house, he discovered
thousands of pieces of leather stuffed behind the lath and plaster as
insulation. He imagined the glovers of Gloversville stealing leftover
bits from the cutting floor, feeding them through slots they cut in their
walls the way during Sunday dinner at his parents' house he snuck
table scraps to his parents' dog. The house was hungry. He thought
about how a finished glove can only keep one hand warm, but their
discards keep warm a whole house. He imagined the calves and kids
killed for the softness of their hides. He imagined the mismatched
shapes in the dark like small animals in their nests, breathing the slow
breath of sleep. He stood alone in the second-floor bedroom
and listened.

FRANCISCO ARAGÓN

Fair Oaks Street

San Francisco

Wooden façade
seems to be saying *You
don't belong here
anymore* Victorian
that birthed you
no longer sees

you—scrawny
buzz cut tank
top brother
sisters grew
up there too
a short walk
from the corner
grocer's *Moony's*
his German
Shepherd
that once
snarled chased
you home your
small sticky
fist releasing
the popsicle

The house sold
—two tony
condos
no garage
decades later
the street
still courses
through you—who
will you take

to see it someday
so you can say
Here is where

ANDREA COHEN

Gust of Wind

In the middle
of the gust

is *us*—what
a thing—to be

blown about,
to be blown

as glass is—
by lips into

a vessel.

ANDREA COHEN

Inverness

Standing beneath the lemon
tree, in summer, in the autumn

of what one calls a life, I
call out—and a deep

valley answers. Why
speak of endings?

It's enough to sit
with all these twilights,

enough to remember
lemons in a blue

afternoon two
people woke to——

ANDREA COHEN

Eurydice

I did
love him—

what's his name,
I mean—

the one
who looked

so handsome
and stricken

looking back.
And that

other one—
who looked

after me
after that

fiasco.

ANDREA COHEN

Web

Inside the spider's web
is what you'll find inside

the spider: everything
that might, by a spider,

be eaten, all the ideas
that fly or crawl in.

It's an old story: eat
or dream of eating.

Even a spider tires
of it, and on six legs

walks away, as if there
might be a seventh

leg on which to rest.

ANDREA COHEN

After Reading Frederick Seidel

I take a bath.
And a shower.

I tell the flowers:
go play outside––

in the traffic
of lust, I mean.

Mean bed, mean
hours, planning

all manner
of ruin without me.

KATHLEEN OSSIP

Music Performed at Night, at a Distance

this is the stranger come to town
they see the quiet, they want to cry
they see a bench and they sit down

these are the blessed drops of rain
this is the rain unsafe to drink
this is the place that's always the same
this is the sameness that drives us insane

this is the thought they're fighting against
this is the thought they'd better not think
this is the muscle that's always tense
this is the song that will now commence

this is the stream dyed sick and pink
this is the rain that made it clear
is this the end you always feared

this is the logic of this hates that
this is the dream that circled the sink
this is the whisper that told us of
the tundra that's dying from fault of love

the whisper that chokes in a dying fall
to hide an emotion unsure and small
to hide that there is no emotion at all

here are the forest trees creeping in

this is the logic of purpose and use
this is the logic of setting the mood
this is the logic of buy me this
this is the logic of what in the world

this is the kite we thought was a drone
this is the bingewatch that knits up the nerves

this is the only return that we'll get

we listen to music performed at night
this is the bandshell in brilliant light
this is the sanitization machine
this is the story we wanted wiped clean

only a game it was only a game
this is the thought we're fighting against
this is the jenga that never collapsed
that stood on the table inside the estate

because of the quiet it never collapsed

when is the filter a bad mistake
app in the folder taking up space
when is the fabric rubbed the wrong way
who will the troopers tear awake

this is the sandwich we ate between shifts
this is the only return that we'll get

this is the hatred of the small
this is the rose without a bloom
bought from the kiosk in the mall
where we drove when we tired of our room

here is the stranger who sees a sign
wandering around and counting time
with a rose in one hand and feet that ache
the sense we fear is the sense we make

this is the song the stranger heard
this is the message the stranger wrote
these are the blessed drops of rain
this is the meme that makes it plain

KATHLEEN OSSIP

Bird

West 261st Street

The few times I submerged
in a rough wave, capsized and
freeform in a jellied world,

shriekless in a new element:
Was it like that?
The boy shook his head

and ran to his house.
"I have to get a paper towel!"
Maybe he gave it a funeral.

Blue ablution. Blue fact
just barely. No more
than two inches long,

squashed on impact. It had
no feathers. Transparent, smoke-blue
skin, or casing, immaterial as scum,

contained its organs. Thread legs,
infinitesimal tined feet. Head
the size of an unripe berry

bulged with veins and brain.
The kid in black shorts, white tee, Nikes,
eight years old?, stood a block

away, pointed to a spot
on the sidewalk and screamed.
Screamed almost a pure musical note.

Looked around and screamed again.
This time performing surprise or alarm.
He posed for a reaction, keen

to be seen. We all are.
Half a block away, I called
"What's wrong?" As I approached—

"A mother bird dropped her baby from the nest."
His voice was forthright
as an angel guarding Eden.

It grounded the image. He wasn't shocked.
He pointed. The words came true
and then I looked and saw.

DAVID BLAIR

Two Shorts

1. The Sheriff of Good Poetry

        You're pulled over in the breakdown lane

on the highway after driving too fast
through the marshes famous
for their North Shore painterly light

not too far past the Alfalfa Farm, uninspected,
the registration two months out of date. Oh no. The sheriff of good
poetry is explaining to you how you need this good book. It's good
for you. It hides your face. It's a form of ragout when you are hungry.
On the other hand, sometimes the sheriff is out there directing traffic,
pointing, whistling, handing out more broadsides than tickets, cita-
tions, a pain, some blood-orange moon fingerprints and white gloves.
Dorito breath. The dispenser of the state and institutions. You can do
a month inside, tops.

2. The Raven That Shits on Poets

—in memory of Charles Simic

        Just as I finished the book on the park bench, a crow in the lin-
den tree spattered my left blue sleeve and wrist with drips and streaks
of white water practically, the lightest touch. Sorry, not sorry, says
Charlie. There was that rip in the side of the bulkie roll package at
the cold counter about the width of the head of something furry using
its Köpfen-shape. The rat has a dream, too: a helmet and facemask
of bread. Mt. Palmolive. The gift there. You're soaking in dish soap.
Break out some aspergillum in the bushes, you bums. That was no
Bishop of Secrecy passed over the trestle with smiling pigs on the side
of the train, cold bacon inside. In the sunlit rain.

Untitled 1

LAUREN ALLEYNE

Immigrant Duplex

For Douglas Kearney. After Jericho Brown.

What questions might the world ask of me
after I have buried myself whole?

I have buried myself in the hole
of America, its plastic freedoms,

elastic unfreeness—America,
you have rendered me a corpse of delightful

emptiness. You have plundered me of heft,
ground the God in me to tin and clatter.

God, the grind. The death din and rattle
of markets, marching—everything for sale,

marked. I bought my own drum to march to;
it hangs around my neck like a price tag

made of history. My neck stuck out for no one,
what questions might the world ask of me?

LAUREN ALLEYNE

Writer's Block

What poetry to write
this bloody morning
with its snipers and
handcuffed students,
with its foreign dead,
with its hungry cancer
eating your friend's
bones, with the bones
of children unearthed
from a Palestinian mass
grave, with the planet's
rising human-fed fever,
with your mother's voice
crackling with pain
across the long distance
call, with the masses
in you feeding themselves
on your stocked up griefs,
with the words squeezed
into silences so dense
they crush you—alphabet,
throat and song?

MOLLY TWOMEY

Gnawed to Bone

I swung a pineapple
    by its mohawk,
burst a melon on lino.

Granted, I was dreaming
    but I know the panic
when what I need

is out of stock.
    My body has shrunk
behind the cage of a trolley,

afraid to approach
    what is trapped under
bar codes. On my birthday

I fractured my ankle
    kicking the car boot
as I filled it. I want to hold

the girl scrutinizing
    yogurt rice cakes,
pistachios detained in shells.

Her calorie tracker open,
    nails breaking through
the scalp of a cantaloupe.

Seven years in recovery.
    All I crave is a lit match
to throw at the grocery store.

MOLLY TWOMEY

At the Guggenheim, Venice

After Pegeen Vail Guggenheim

Yours is a future I work
to avoid, a palette of valium,
a bath of open skin.

I don't want my love to think he exists
to keep my blood flowing.
Would you have painted all this

if you'd been skinny dipping in Lido,
sharing *Fritole* and *Amarone*?
I am lost in this shrine

of pastel and gouache,
tiny waists and tight wristbands
like blacked-out text.

If I could, I would pick an escape hatch
in your vitrine, unseal the dank basement
you locked yourself in to create.

MOLLY TWOMEY

I Ask Levenshulme High School Girls What Boils Their Blood

Islamophobia, they reply,
and buttons that fall off shirts.

Old people, one girl adds and later clears up
that her grandmother won't stop pinching
the plush toy of her stomach.

People who piss about while others get hurt,
says a girl cradling her wrist
in a cast of Sharpie hearts.

How many nights have I insisted
'text when you get home'
only to make a cup of chamomile,

watch Gossip Girl, my phone unchecked,
my windows locked behind blackout curtains?
Unsolicited advice, says a voice at the back,

reapplying her contraband lip balm.
I swallow warnings to always carry
a hatpin or the sharp tail of a comb,

that wearing dungarees buys you time.
I ask what they're obsessed with—
half-zips, chicken tenders, hair brushes that don't break.

One girl says she is happier the farther she gets
from her home. Another loves dancing
behind a locked door to The Smiths and Lana Del Rey.

I dream a future where none of them ever drags
back the morning to see their blood
swept up, torn skirts lifted and binned.

Their stories, slips of paper
that never get typed, drifting over
St Peter's Square, the tram tracks, the crypt.

MATTHEW GREENFIELD

Migraine

Omens — filaments
Of shadow webbing at the
  Edges of objects.

The after-image
Of a flash-bulb: an absence.
  Visible darkness.

Then the unearthly
Colors, the throbbing haloes:
  Mint, pearl, lavender.

Again the fortress
High in the air, sparks spilling
  From its bright turrets.

A penumbra of
Non-feeling around the pain's
  Precise little stab.

The transfiguring
Rich agony of the saint.
  The self, deepening.

MATTHEW GREENFIELD

Plutonium

You glow invisibly,
But you seem heavy and dull,
    Like the lead you will become.

You have a long half-life,
With too much time to think.
    You are married to quietness.

The red stain at her mouth
Is the only color here,
    The color of a bleeding fruit.

Above, the small, cold planet
Pursues its eccentric path,
    Undetected. No one

Is born under its sign.

MATTHEW GREENFIELD

Ovid

It has a hundred mouths —
One with its lips on a flute,
One tongueless, drooling blood;
A mouth with a human song,
A mouth with the song of a bird,
And a mouth that sounds like a river;
A mouth that repeats the words and the cries
Of all of the other mouths,
A mouth that refuses to utter
Anything but its own name,
And a mouth that tears off and swallows
The flesh of its own body.

It has two light-boned wings
And a single pale flower
As soft as the throat of a girl.
Some of its parts have been flayed;
Others are clenched in ecstasy.

On a beach by a darkening ocean
A simpler body walks.
In the cold air, his breath
Unfurls like a sequence of scrolls.

He hopes that when he dies
He will be transformed to a star
Without a voice or body.

MATTHEW GREENFIELD

Locust Trees

When you cut them down, those nets of root
Refuse to die — they come up out of the dark

All over the lawn. In three months
They are as tall as men, but spindly, too weak

To need more than one stroke of a dull scythe.
The second year some of them try again,

And the third year you might get one or two.
The roots may persist longer, in the cool dark.

If you were to dig up a part that lived
And put it in good soil with water,

It might rise up into the light
As if it were going to survive.

MATTHEW GREENFIELD

Nova Scotia

In the dim harbor, in a house on stilts,
A lantern lights its small crazed window-pane.

An empty feather bed, remembrance quilts,
A stoneware crock rough-fired in salt, a stain

On the ceiling, a clean bare floor. Snow falls
On the spruce trees and into the dark stream

Whose mouth is here. These presences seem
Shrouded, sealed in nimbus or caul

EILEEN CLEARY

I Spoke with a Deer by Winter and Holly Ridge,

mid-day, while my rescue dog: fawn-tinged, cervine,
stood mute, and to my surprise, discreet in the way

she paused, her head still, poised as a reading table,
her eyes set to deer, the deer transfixed

near the curb. Did she grok my desire? Her well-being.
At ease, the doe sought no leaf litter. No camouflage tree.

No unlit shadow to outshadow her underbelly.
One must talk to deer as if they are a painting,

only without the benefit of tombstone labels.
The artist can see you in the masterpiece.

Like any good artist he has vanished.
Let imagination finish. I do.

The deer knows my hard night at work, knows
I'm walking off another hard luck story.

A quarter mile down the road,
the Cape house I folded from paper

has outlasted thirty years of rain.
I'm writing a lullaby

for a bright-eyed girl with lilacs on her romper.
May she never have to outrun her heart.

I am thinking of Miguel Hernández, imprisoned
while his wife subsisted on onion skins,

his son on onion milk,
how the larks of his house once knew orange blossoms,

how his dark-haired wife emptied her
moons into the cradle. If only.

The deer knows my naive aim to tame hunger.
Today, the deer translates me to myself.

Says my name means light,
that for this minute, she is none of my dead.

ELLE CHU

youngwon

disrespectfully, i call you into this poem
by first name. i hope you understand
there is no other way to start talking
about you, though i do know how i
am supposed to talk to you.

though we believe we have nothing else to exchange
except small, casual gifts of seasonal fruit, we painfully share
a joke over the kitchen sink: my berry-stained mouth
a more vibrant red than your careful made-up lip.
i have laughs i've stored up for moments like these,
because again, you trap me in your mourning of how american i am
and how it must be the influence of my pittsburgh daddy
that i walk unlike a lady, eat unlike a lady, and i at least
smell like a lady — but not in the good way. it doesn't matter
how i respond. you tell me how your fancy scholars' dinner went
by showing a picture on your phone that looks like
all the other photographs you're throwing out. you say
many of your friends came to celebrate your academic contributions.
because you're a very important person. which leads to a rare honesty:
you're old and tired of these dinners, but you hate the idea
of being forgotten even more. it's then that i realize your honesty
comes with a price: you want me to offer to write your memoir
because your death is anticipated. your death is respectable
because your life needs to be remembered.

my death — even talking about it — would be an act of disrespect.
as i am not allowed to die before my ancestors,
you push영원 off the plaque you were awarded
into my squirming american mouth.

my clumsy tongue, grown out of its cuteness, struggles to hold onto the grace
of a grandmother looking onto her english-speaking grandchild.
you tell me your name means the same thing as forever, sort of.
i don't know how to explain to you that i don't write in korean

and all my english poetry starts with the idea of containers
and i cannot write the story of a grandmother who's more interested
in being honored than being loved. or maybe she thinks they are the same.
either way, she doesn't know enough english
to ask me to write her into immortality.

and thank God because while i hide my reluctance
behind my teeth and the berry's pulp, i cannot stand
that i understand her request. and even more, i cannot stand
that i yearn to protect her eternal self from living on
some english page in some english paragraph
where only some of who she is and all of who she's hurt
will not make sense to her. she falls in love
with every celebrated version of herself, but what if she sees
that i love the memory of my written grandmother more?
what will happen to the grandmother in front of me?
i might as well die with her name in my mouth.

TOM DALEY

Psalm: The Man Who Walked Naked in My Little Apartment in Carrboro

You are He who treads
down the desire of the wicked,

yet why do You still
awake for me

the deranging passion
for the loins

of the man who was my friend?
Judge me not, O Lord,

who makes the stars chaste,
when I train my eyes

on that apparatus destined
for the depositing

of the seed of man
in the fertile place

where woman grows
our replacements.

If I establish his image
in that part of my mind

reserved for a fruitful
desire, know that I am a bent

arrow finding my way
to my own sex.

My desire is my mischief.
My heart is a ditch,

a trench filled with the caterwaul
of his parade,

where he, of proportions
perfect and righteous,

swung his greatness
over the wall-to-wall carpet

of my studio apartment
as he unfolded his sleeping bag

on nights when it was too cold
to return to the unheated house

he was constructing
in the woods

of Pittsboro. He knew nothing
of how my eyes roasted

the springload
of his tightening buttocks,

how I ranged my tastebuds
in my ignorant imagination

over the skin
that traversed the cockpit

of his fecund place and traveled
down half the length of his pride.

PATRICK COTTER

On Pruning and Other Matters

The man with a tree rising out of his head stopped
feeling guilty for his talent long ago, the gift he'd never
earned, never asked for. The one he was born with.

You believe I'm special, he'd think to himself, *but I'm only
you with my head growing a tree.* People in town squares
would throw coins at him, pin banknotes to his twigs

while he just stood there. During the season his tree fruited
childless women plead with him to fill their wombs, often
holding their husband's hand as they presented their petition.

Does it hurt to have your berries plucked? a boy once enquired.
Only when they're still green. He'd wander from town to town
all through the climate-varied continent, trying to keep one step

ahead of autumn and its leaf-stripping powers. Occasionally
he would seek out a tree-surgeon. Nothing could prevent
pruning from hurting, no drugs, only skill could lessen it.

But without prudent clipping the branches would grow
too large to let him slip through doors or properly rest his head.
Once a bonsai master told him *The things I could do for you*

without ever elaborating. Treeman scoffed and moved
on to the next town, leaving a pair of sparrows flying overhead
searching for their missing, cheeping nest, bills full of mayflies.

PATRICK COTTER

Like Prisons, Our Own Gifts

The boy under whose bed a forest rumbled could not slide
asleep without listening to the mournful hooting of owls
the howling of wolves – all at such a soft calming volume

since the critters needed to be teeny enough to dwell in a forest
sprouting under a boy's bed, a forest never shedding its leaves
despite the permanent darkness and dearth of rain. In certain

seasons he could thrust his hand inside and apples the size
of regular apple seed peppered into his palms, tarting his mouth
as any rare variety when chomped by the handful. He kept

the cleanest room of any boy, so his mother had no excuse for rushing
in, scouring under his bed, discovering the forest, sweeping it away
with sperm-crusted socks. He never stayed out all night, stayed in weekends.

All his nightmares dramatised a forest being scooped up, plopped
in an ash bin. Miniature deer, owls, wild pigs and wolves, apple trees
elms, oak, sycamore – all engulfed by the housefire's light, sterile leavings.

Binmen carting away his world to a putrid landfill to be snaffled
by monstrous rats and ravenous seagulls roaming far from the sea.
Leaving his underbed a tomb, his soul a derelict site of seclusion.

NINA MACLAUGHLIN

Green

Autumn equinox and the green gives way. From a train along the coast between Boston and New York, first sighting of the change, a magenta taking hold of the leaves on low trees I could not identify. Snowy egret in the marsh grass somewhere in Connecticut. Empty osprey nest on a telephone poll over a lapping bay on the eastern edge of this continent. Someone said in conversation recently, "of course the coastline is fractal," as if every idiot is supposed to know. By fractal in this case, did he mean unmeasurable? What can we measure? The distance between two cities. The number of hours of daylight. The headlines announced last week that there are three billion fewer birds around than there were fifty years ago. I don't know how they measure this but I can't stop thinking about all the wings. The dead birds, three billion of them, in a feathered heap in a crater pit somewhere in Arizona. September brings the yellow, and the fuzzed plants burst and take the light and throw it at us as some sort of undeserved reward.

NINA MACLAUGHLIN

Jaws of Life

It rained all night.
The air is thick now.
The brothers are in the garden.
The small brother is by the peonies,
pink and white and slumped low,
too heavy for themselves,
about to bow under the weight
of their own exuberance.
The small brother,
in a light blue shirt,
takes the stem of one of the flowers
and shakes it. He is gentle.
He turns to see where his brother is,
wants him to see what is happening,
wants him to know
how he relieves the flowers,
how they are not slumped and sad now
with the weight of all the rainwater.
The larger brother has been watching
the whole time, crouched near a bed
of zucchini vines, and when his brother
turns to look for him, he pretends
to be absorbed in a Japanese beetle.
Their mother had urged them outside.
Good rainbow-hunting weather, she had said.
Last night, the smaller brother had fallen
asleep in a chair and the larger brother
watched as his mother, her hair loose,
wearing a long blue skirt and a thin white shirt,
bent to scoop the sleeping brother into her arms,
and the bones of her spine stegged
against her shirt as she did.
The small brother's legs dangled
over her arms, his quiet, sleeping face
pressed into her neck like soft fruit.

I will walk my own self to bed, the larger brother thought.
I am too large now to be loved this way.
"Toad," the larger brother calls out
in the garden, and the smaller brother
rushes across the mulch path to where
his brother crouches. "There," he says.
"I see it," says the smaller brother,
getting down on his knees.
The toad, no bigger than a cherry,
speckled brown and dark green,
a tiny animal mud puddle,
stands still by the corner of the zucchini bed,
a bulldogging posture speaks its fear.
The toad's body swells and deflates
as it fills and empties its tiny lungs,
then it seems not to breathe at all.

The larger brother in a yellow and red
striped shirt pulls a twig from the mulch
and pokes the toad's back.
"Don't," says the smaller brother.
He does it again, pressing harder.
The toad's flesh gives under the twig.
"Don't. They don't like it."
The larger brother stands, breaks the twig
in half and flings the pieces toward the fence.

"One Two Three," he says.
A game the brothers play:
one holds the wrist of the other
and on the count of three,
begins to bend his first finger back,
slowly, as far as possible, to see
how far it can go without the other
calling out "jaws of life!"
which means stop, and the finger is released.

The smaller brother stands
and offers his wrist to his brother.

The larger brother grabs his wrist
in one hand and takes hold
of the index finger with the other
and they look into each other's eyes.
The larger brother counts. Then
begins the slow pressing back,
bending the index finger toward
the public part of the wrist,
against the way it wants to go.

The smaller brother smiles, the thrill
of it not hurting yet, knowing it will hurt.
The larger brother feels himself
gripping his brother's wrist harder,
and becomes aware of his back teeth
as he clenches his jaw.
The smaller brother squirms
across his shoulders and stamps
his right foot in the mulch.
He starts to hum, a high hum
in the back of his throat,
which they both know means
he's getting close to shouting.
The larger brother, slowly,
slowly, tiny finger in his hand,
presses deeper, staring
his small brother in the face.
A crow lands on the ridgeline
of the shed. A dragonfly with tiny rainbows
caught in the iridescent net of its wings
hovers by a fencepost, flies off into the trees.

"Jaws of life!" the smaller brother shouts.

But instead of letting go,
as are the rules,
the sacred pact,
the magic words,
the larger brother narrows his eyes

and in a flash, action before thought,
jams his brother's finger back, hard,
and his brother makes an animal scream,
and pulls his hand away to his chest
and the look he gives his larger brother
will live in the larger brother's mind
for the rest of his years on earth,
and every time it appears,
he will feel a sick and cringing sorrow
as he then pictures his brother
holding his hand to his chest, eyes wet,
walking to the far side of the shed
to cry in the shade alone.

TINA CANE

Faire Simple

It's so much simpler to be hurt than to hurt   Samuel Beckett observed after James Joyce

paid him for work on his proofs with a few French sous and a hand-me-down overcoat   no phone call

on my birthday from my Marine Corps dad made this year no different from the last except for the fact

that we're recently in touch and have been speaking each week these past several months   I'm old enough

now to confess I wanted a message from my dad marking my too-early arrival into this world unwilling still

for this flicker of disappointment to mar our correspondence   for despondence is a choice so I choose

to voice my grievance on the page for that particular Saturday in June was mild with a hint of sun striving

from behind a haze of clouds fortuitous how Father's Day fell right after so I had to reflect on what it means

that my birthstone changes red to green *emerald by day ruby by night* they say depending on the light

my black hair hangs like a shadow at my shoulder or like a folded wing sometimes *alexandrite* embodies Mercury

of myth swift messenger often tasked with bearing bad news   all this to say sorry I had to tell you you are not

mine please know I was a *mercurial* child a teenager later fraught and wild   I used to say *Pourquoi faire simple*

quand on peut faire compliqué? but time changes everything   my heart is greener than it's ever been

TINA CANE

To Be Human Is to Contain Plastic

Does every man die calling for his mother and every mother perish with fuel

in her breast to be human is to contain plastic to be plastic is to never degrade

the administrator at the V.A. asks my father for his dates by which she means

his tours of duty in the war   *You mean, the killing?* he says I'm not aiming

to be impertinent he adds that's just what it was: fields covered in blood jungle rot

that does not resolve ghosts who never recede

                                        we speak on the phone each week

my dad and me reflexively circling back over the same terrain: my children his service

how much he loves chicken chow mein the way Woodstock remains a drunken blur

the many names and dates that continue to elude even as our neuroplasticity expands into

an unspoken language we share but a handful of memories with fifty years lost between

them and now it's become extraneous that we aren't joined by blood like he and my mother

believed still our hearts go on continuously scarred by brightly colored bits lodged in chambers

flecked with plastic *micro nano* imperceptible traces we meld into our systems each day a new

communion of refuse or refusal to rid a bid to stick with this   even as it kills every one of us

CHRISTINE JONES

from *Limb of Water*

silver plankton

kick   kick

broken shore

its disappearing
waist

eons before
our time

the roseate tern

the hypothermic terrapin

the horseshoe crab
445 million years old

step aside!

their voices clear

through
the veil

I was thinking   Ocean

what you must think of us
within this green-gray existence

swimming the shallows

drunk on bottomless
mimosas

I don't intimately know

        the soft-bodied nautilus buried

    beneath the fluted sand

   in its glass-spiraled
     chamber
          not been

  under a hunter's moon

     nor followed

           the coyote's dark-lit paws

   to the thicket thick in the marsh

where no humans tread
           without

    a moonglade to meet death

            I am waiting

  kick kick

    crests   froth

 a salutation

  or a snarl?

a buoy

its barnacles

its rusted clasp

rope dis-
enfranchised

bobbing with the picked-up
wind

RICHARD HOFFMAN

Meditation

Even when the surface is smooth,
reflecting trees and clouds, the river
is a rock-braided churning syntax
trout hold themselves in, steady,
having found, by feel, their haven.
Sometimes music helps remind me,
wordlessly, where I belong, where
I wait for something to come to me,
waiting being it seems my fortune,
here amid changing time signatures,
where one day I'll be swept away.
It is knowing that that steadies me
in flashing light and moving shade,
a constant effort but with peace in it.

RICHARD HOFFMAN

Pax Americana

As far as I can tell the empire's still the crucified
as far as the eye can see, hectares of crosses
both sides of the road, their anguish bound
for distribution to the cities and dope-sick towns
that turn to gray stone and enlistment bonuses.

Now rows of solar panels in the stolen fields,
both sides of the road, in a sodden week of rain,
word of another friend's overdosed daughter,
and mine so hurt she can only wail long syllables
trying to tell me what's just happened to her life.

And on the same road, but far from here, trucks
as far as the eye can see hold food and medicine
for refugees and are refused by men well-armed
with crude maps of a future world: this one's
done for, as far as I can tell; it died of cruelty.

As far as I can tell centurions still gamble: who,
in which field, which row, accused of god knows
what, will be first to succumb, and the women
will be forced to carry the war to term again
and be responsible for cleaning it all up afterward.

Everything's like looking through a dirty window,
no let up in sight the rain not washing anything.
Soldiers turn children to meat and bloody rags,
take off their helmets and, thumbs up, snap a selfie
that ends up in a magazine about investments.

On both sides of the road there are walls going up
that at home in the empire most are grateful for
since what is done with our tribute hurts to hear:
high tension lines from the fields of crosses hum,
and echoing hammers ring, building god knows what.

ELAINE JOHANSON

Girl Reading a Letter, Restored

fig. 1

Natalie sits in the light

of the Dutch masters, which is clear
but not cold, which comes through
the window without restraint or aggression.

She's scrolling through messages from her lover,
who communicates by emoji. She texts,
"I desire you." He rolls on the floor, laughing.

We humor her. She loves him.
She touches her hair in recognizable,
rinsed milk light.

*

In Dresden, x-rays have exposed the lie
within the Vermeer: the paint concealing
Cupid wasn't his but another's

attempt at revision. We loved it.
We were wrong. He intended for the fat baby
to lord over her shoulder.

Day after day, a conservator scrapes
overpaint off the cracked, immaculate cheek
with a microscope and scalpel,

to our disappointment. We liked ourselves
better as her confidantes, and she
as blank as the wall. Yet

the painting glows now: deep brown
to balance green, sun centering
on her profile, and that blue! Its brightness

reconcentrating on the window frame,
the bunched tapestry, the pale, luminous walls.
Vermeer bankrupted himself in fidelity

to that clarity of light, its brilliant
undertone created by crushing
lapis lazuli into a transparent glaze.

It's a blue you can fall into, that you
can be stupid for, like the early spring
evenings in Paris so clear no god

of love could hide itself,
cobalt pooling lushly around anything
that glows. And isn't that true

here, too? How, in the wreckage
of her desire, what I see
is my friend slowly revealing

herself to herself, how light
concentrates what radiates already,
here in the sea-lit room.

*

fig. 2

It's quiet here, where water threatens.
The dark sky lowers itself
over still canals. We hurry

back through the cold, the heat
of the pub leaving our bodies
at the same rate as we build it

in ourselves, between ourselves, chattering,
a warmth you would paint in yellow lake,
vermillion, umber, verdigris, and all of it

incandescent with rare ultramarine.

ELAINE JOHANSON

The Heat Death of the Universe

I hate the phrase, "It is what it is."
"But sometimes it's true," you say,

like the universe's inherent laws. Case in point:
there is never less chaos. Each thought hurries the stars' dissolution.

And at the end of that? It's the coldest day
in years. Salt dries in white bursts on the parking lot. We crack

icy oysters and pour them into our mouths to taste some faraway bay
while you tell me about the newly launched James Webb Telescope, how

for months it has to chill with its face turned from the sun. Only then
will it reflect the faint waves that remain from the first

spasm of stars. The hope? That the end will blush within
the beginning, though certainty is almost certainly beyond

our lifetimes, still. Forty, now, we wake again and again, knotted
in the shadowy bed. Will I watch you age? I never considered it,

young enough not to live grief before grief. But now "I want
my particles to be close to your particles," I joke, though by the time

the universe spreads to frozen equilibrium, we won't even be that.
There's comfort in cosmic time, its cartoon length. Comfort, too,

in grasping at each moment as it twists by, trying to pause
the curve of your neck bending to shell, the brine sting,

the candles' spreading gold. *Stop, stop* as we hurtle apart, warming
each other ever closer toward our still and radiant end.

After the Curtain Went Down

"Lucia has Joyce's enthusiasm, energy,
and a not-yet-determined amount of his genius.
When she reaches her full capacity
for rhythmic dancing, James Joyce
may yet be known as his daughter's father."
—*Paris Times*

After four years of ceaseless practice.
After three apprenticeships and a role

as a little soldier in a Jean Renoir film.
After all the arabesques and perfect

angles assigned by Isadora Duncan's
brother and months on the road

with a traveling dance troupe. After
the performance when the *Paris Times*

raved about her art, then Lucia designed
her own costume for the first international

festival of dance and crawled across
the Paris stage—part woman, part fish,

scales shining under the cruel lights.
Beckett and Joyce joined the crowd

as they yelled *give it to the Irish girl*
when she came in second. Then, her body

was no longer her body. Somewhere
in a cafe, benches covered in red velvet,

they convinced her she was not strong
enough to be a dancer of any kind.

When a woman has a fervent mind, the men
around her want to quiet her body. What

determination to discourage does it take
to put out that passion? What commitment

to cruelty to take a body bound to dance
to sit still at a desk to paint lettrines?

What did he promise you to keep
you still? Did you think you would

suddenly share more of his soul?
After a month crying alone above

the lights of Paris. After the curtain
went down and the costumes were boxed

in tissue. After the sepia photographs
were tucked silently in the drawer,

you sit inscrutable, a statue. Silent
as a crossword. Sculpted as a shell.

JENNIFER FRANKLIN

Virginia Woolf is Afraid to Read Proust and Joyce

"Nothing has really happened until it has been described."
                                        —Virginia Woolf

She knows they are all working to achieve
the same thing—to show the way the past
lives inside the present—the taste
of the madeleine, the walk along the Liffey,
the clock striking eleven—her unused hour
and the national grief of armistice.
She was afraid to drown in their words
and not resurface. She was afraid.
So, in these moments she did not see
the genius of her own mind. How horrible
the toll those Duckworth brothers took.
I wish she had used a knife on them—cut
a path to the past so in every present moment,
they would have to remember what they had done.

SUZANNE MERCURY

[Every Word a Poem]

and the mark on

the page

        is a sound :

s'wonderful   s'marvelous

A stainless staining   and a page corner

Left folded   into a transfigured leaf

A mark made

and I am arching my back into a

hyperaesthetic landscape

of words

Sound forgives

you   instantly

it forges its filament

into a unspooling *hiraeth*   ad infinitum

into a break   in the side of

       a mountain

You can light it and see

but only for a moment

      But that is all it takes

to take you into the no place

that sees you   and (made real)

sees you again

KATE PARTRIDGE

Two Children Are Threatened by a Nightingale

after Max Ernst

      The thing is (a blessing),
the gate is already open. Its red arm
      gestures beyond
the frame like a gracious host from the

      universe—one outside
of terror. What does a gate do but let us
      pass or teach us
to climb? You'll see: that woman running

      through the field, a butcher's
knife longer than her arm? She can lay it down.
      The hunched, faceless
man preparing to leap from the roof-

      top out to the cabinet
handle? He'll make it, too. Then, the long-haired child
      abreast in his
arms will, at last, steal the chance to look

      back—how the sky descends
into light, clarity. She will always be
      a person from fear,
but not (thank the nightingale) within it.

KATE PARTRIDGE

Mirage

Unlike the tree stump, band saw
still stuck in its side, I did not refuse
to go. In fact, it seemed to me
the only way—to shatter,
reassemble elsewhere, as the tree
declined to do at the hands
of some (frankly, crappy) sawyer
who thought it should appear hundreds
of miles away for the World's Fair.
Chicago. Already, I was long past
on the left coast, where between
each stoplight on Figueroa someone
recited Keats, not to pass time but
to use it. *Do I wake or sleep?* I
looked back to the mountains
for my self, not shaking (aspens)
but climbing (columbine). Here
I was directing my purple reach
toward sky, adopting the rules
of elevation—more water, sharp
light. In the high desert, the one
persistent radio signal dictates
direction in your thoughts. A program
of bird calls, or the bass-deep
melody of country love. A dedicated
trail leads to the stump's rigid
base, dug out in the little ponderosa
grove. Around, the valley plain
abandoned, coops silent at the farm
where two women read books on
botany, then went out to look.
Standing there, it's clear there
was nothing else to do. Prairie
grass waving. Same birds calling
each other back. Even prairie dogs,

their network below, whistle
warning as you approach. What
is left, really, but to learn
the songs on the dial, to practice
re-assembling the sounds in
your voice—until you become
someone the future might
recognize—as a bird, as wind. As
the truth, perhaps, or even as a lie.

KATE PARTRIDGE

Little Grief

One bite from the world's taut
surface—swallowed—colors
everything for days. Full-bodied
leathery eras. A glass of smoke.

ORLANDO RICARDO MENES

Oration Written While Listening
to Brian Eno's "Slow Water"

Do not let gravity deny my little brook
to flow uphill, rapid as a cataract
in reverse, strident, fearless, whose roar
will crackle the air's atoms to canticles,
whose spray will brink heaven and mingle
with the cumuli that birth easter's rain.
Gravity distorts, topples, dominates,
and the land is complicit in its tyranny:
its maps, titles, and liens hard-etched
to greed, its plats that plot iniquity,
those border stones, chain links, bollard fences
that pilfer the poor's hope and dignity.
Pray for my little brook to maul the soil
into pastels for a seascape because only water
is kinetic and affluent by birthright,
its path skewed to its own will as it sings
with the angels' oboes slushing in ocean winds
and chants alone freedom's obstinate spell.

ORLANDO RICARDO MENES

Hear Me, All Apostates

Let your guilt sink at sea in an iron urn,
and you'll be free to roam the earth—
a saint—naked and unafraid.
Your spit will bless cast-offs,
runaways, addicts, the infirm of mind
and body who beg on roadsides
for a chalice of soup, a patten of bread.
Your hands will knead skin to scripture's grace.
What pride you have left will simmer
in a pot until it succumbs to dross,
leavings of humbleness to scatter
on the innocent dead, the migrants dried
to husk in the desert, iced in a plane's wheel-
well, or drowned in Styrofoam rafts
with bedsheet sails, those nameless hundreds
caught in storms or snagged by billows,
my kindred Cubans and Haitians too,
the Rohingyas, Syrians, and Senegalese,
who wash ashore unseen for days or weeks
with their sewn prayers, flotsam pleas.

ORLANDO RICARDO MENES

Pastoral

We are here at Finisterre—the end
of the world—to persevere because
miracles can happen, you say,
where waves surge against the rocks
and homely skies overcast to ash,
which is the color of hope, and only hope
can alter discord to harmony as winds
might weave wildflowers to tapestries.
Come kiss me, you say, in the mist
of dawn's cobalt light and make vows
beneath a fractured moon. But will we
return to Eden in our hearts and minds?
Unlike animals we are not born to purity.
These cows in their barn are free of rancor,
while we bicker as if gravity had pulled us
toward strife against our will. What hope
is there to tame resentment, to appease rage
regular as the sun? Look around, you say,
air, water, and light will heal us, for nature
is more forgiving than God Himself.
No, my love, we humans have no right
to her grace, so many centuries of razing
her forests, slaughtering her beasts,
poisoning every lake and ocean. We must
repent and think not of ourselves but the stray things—
the abandoned, the sick, and the maimed—
and on this dark river that wavers into the sea,
we should tend the castoffs, the orphans,
and the hapless, those skiffs and dories
more abused than dray horses, and thus release
them to the waves, praying they meander
to some graceful harbor and be nursed back to health,
which to a boat means being useful to the end.

HALYNA KRUK

shut out music, as if music were something terrible

shut out music, as if music were something terrible
as if it might enter and steal her soul
then tune that stolen soul to itself
run its fingers through its hair
press on all the soft spots, cause it pain
take root, grow, rip it apart from the inside
remind us that none of us belongs to ourselves
in this reality, in this brutal time
music explodes in our temples
music runs from our wounds,
music pulses,
music ends
and it gets so quiet, as if all she had
was this unbearable music

translated by Ali Kinsella & Dzvinia Orlowsky

HALYNA KRUK

a woman with a heart this heavy cannot fly

a woman with a heart this heavy cannot fly
like a leaf held to asphalt by a rock
like a page from a book disassembled into quotes. . .
a few minutes for meetings, a few snatched words for introductions
her eyes wide open like the door to her parents' house
where all her childhood memories are kept in an old marshmallow tin
she says, "if not him, then no one will get them. . ."
the black butterfly of despair, the sharp smell of ether
who will revive her, return her to her passport photo
who will hold her thin, sobbing shoulders

the air raid siren lifts city birds into the air
but that heaviest thing in her doesn't allow for flight

translated by Ali Kinsella & Dzvinia Orlowsky

HALYNA KRUK

you say when the water recedes our eyes will be dry

you say when the water recedes our eyes will be dry
and silenced words will get stuck in the back of our throats
someone will enter our houses
and carry down from the attics the bodies swollen like bread in water

the upper story is where God's work was to be done
most of those who were born to die on this earth
believed in you, Lord, and that their death
wouldn't be so terrible

you say, eat my flesh, drink my blood
bury your dead in the muck of memory, the sludge of the soul
eternal life begins where
love clung to the edge of the roof
where along the bank between living and dead
the bulrushes will stand as an eternal rebuke

you'll return, Lord, for each of them, right? each of us?
will you send each of us the dove of peace with its olive branch?
our eyes are blind with wrath and despair, staring into time:
so much sank or emerged at once

the mustard seed of faith, Cossack church's cross
mercy, double bottom

translated by Ali Kinsella & Dzvinia Orlowsky

The Eternal Sun

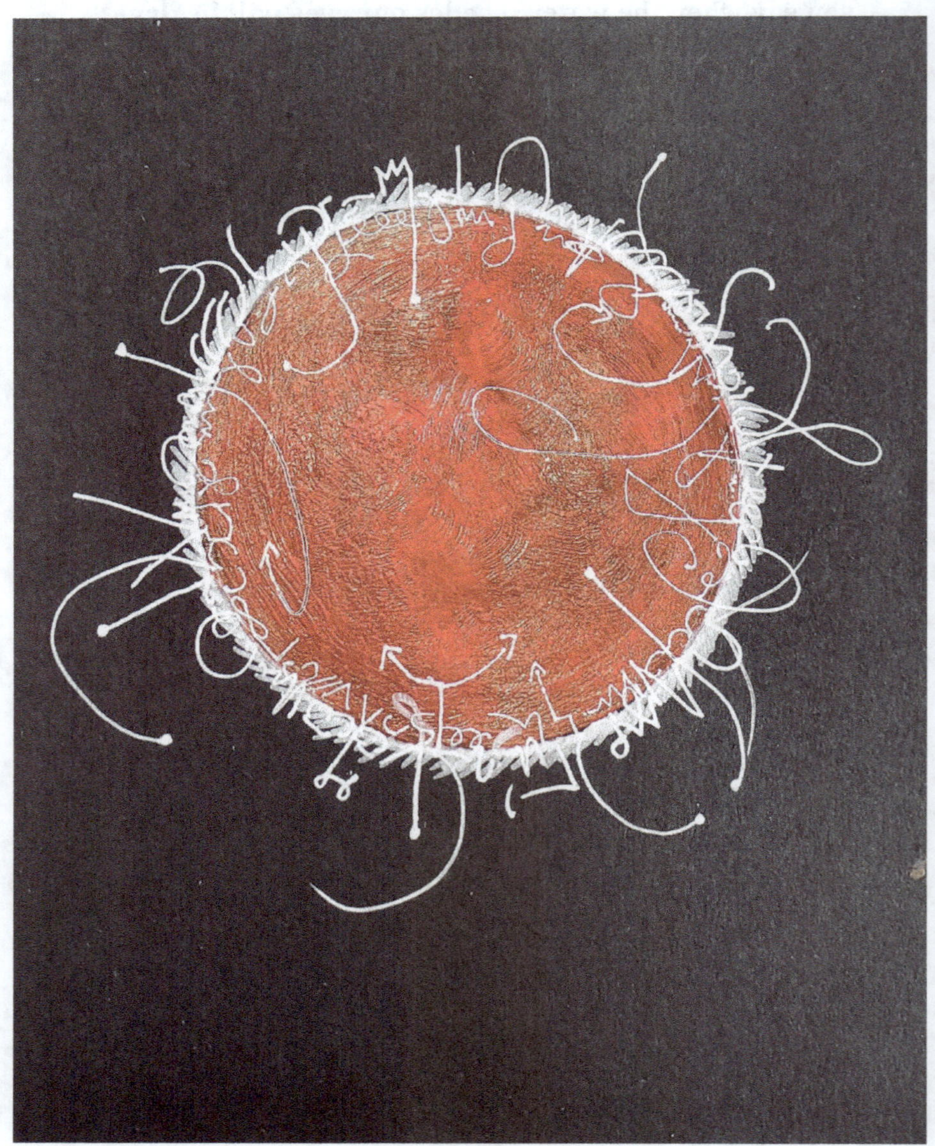

JENNIFER MARTELLI

Rilke

Long ago, my dinner plates were thick glass that shone green in a certain light.

They were fired with white spirals, like frost across a windshield.

I forced my friends to listen to me at my kitchen table, made longer with fold-out wings.

I read Rilke's poem about the angel who wrestles Jacob until he lay sore, still.

Back then, we had angels like John Travolta and Nic Cage, wings furled under coats.

The angels smoked, went into heat, fell in love, fell from heaven, left swirls of feathers.

They envied us, with all our hungers, our death.

We wanted to believe that our suffering was enviable, graceful, necessary.

I served my friends cold grapes, raw fish, pepper salad. Read my Rilke.

I can't remember which translation, though.

Bly's: *this is how he grows, by being defeated decisively by constantly greater beings.*

Snow's: *his growth is: to be deeply defeated by ever-greater beings.*

I can't speak for fidelity to another language or another life.

Fall lasts long past the equinox: it spirals out into the night.

HOWIE FAERSTEIN

I Had To Use a Shovel For I Couldn't Lift It in My Arms

—for Gerald Stern

Out my front
door days after
Jerry's death
or was it the same
day or days before
retrieving morning
paper sprawled over median
stripe raccoon size of
a yearling bear
blood staining
striped tail yellow
double-lines

One-time neighbor
deaf-mute Ted
stopped his car shook
his head pounded his
chest with his good right
hand as we do
in synagogue
on the High Holy Days

Blowflies first
on the shoulder
hovering then feeding
frenzied turkey
vultures joined by black
vultures tearing
chunks of
matted flesh
Maybe it *was* the very
day he died

not that it matters
raccoon dead
music still playing
Jerry singing
All of Me
never dead

J.J. STARR

When I touch my place of ruin

I think of those mountains
gathering

at their dust ruffle,
in whose trees

I made my praise
to the expected

blessings: spring, grief,
the returning birds. Morning

lit the mountain skyline
and ringed the western

edge of Venus's pink
belt, all common

as a comma,
in fact,

it was
a comma,

slipped
between

the dependent clauses
of day and night.

J.J. STARR

Anti-twilight

Alone having walked
the graveled drive

and consumed my after-
noon with yardwork

in this heat, which will not
break for weeks, I

pause in the frame
of the mudroom door

looking up
to the heavy boughs

of the locust tree, and beyond
them, the dusk

smolders a rose wreathe
spreading on the east horizon

as a bowl of light submerges
under the western rim

of the same urn.
The breeze, sighing

as a lover might sigh against
the quiet of a night-struck

bedroom, breaks in the tides
of cicadas whose husked

skins pile in the softest
grass beneath the locust tree.

ALYSE KNORR

Chemical Pregnancy

The life—if you'll allow it—I harbored for exactly three days
crushed itself red and ran down my legs. Three days is nothing:
compare and compare, outline the pros, cheer up and see the sunflowers

downtown, where a museum marks Van Gogh's birthday with
a "spectacular sensory experience." What scrap of mourning
am I allowed? It took Jesus three days to rise. Three days enough time

for the wife to order a gift that will stay in its Amazon box on the shelf
forever. Three days abstaining from wine, three days imagining.
Now: next month. Next month. The word *barren* orbits redly

in my mind. They called it "chemical"—as opposed to "physical"?
But it lived once, physically, as a set of neurons in my mind:
thin white strands interwoven like a tiny seedling's roots.

ALYSE KNORR

Where You Are When You Are Not Here

The science says a thought
        is not a thing and not a place—

not an item but a charge.
        Language, though, I

imagine stored up
        word by word in bytes

in my brain, each on a shelf
        I plunder with my clumsy

sentences, trying, again,
        the transmutation of speech.

When I was a girl I changed
        as I changed: painting rocks

with animals, building stick forts,
        and, once, mummifying a Barbie

after I read a book on old Egypt.
        I understood, at ten and now,

how the mind might leave the body
        through any point of exit—

pulled from a nostril by an embalmer's
        steady tool; leaked out by a lonely

glance; or flown forth, exposed,
        on the gusts of a clumsy tongue.

I have said things without thinking and
        I have thought things without saying:

which is the greater sin? But here I arrive
        at the thought of you. Here

I pick up your name.
        How gentle it feels

in my hands, like a treasure
        just unearthed.

Yes, you are the treasure
        and you are the map

and you are the empty space.
        You are the charge

and the new ancient story—
        everywhere is not a place.

KIRUN KAPUR

Ghazal in a Time of Plague

At dawn, the grackles have discovered something they must say to you.
I slip from bed. Lay out two cups. Old habit: prepare Earl Grey for you.

These years of plague, these years of loving who we love through screens—
Now even the most desperate heart straps on a mask to pray to you.

The storm clouds scroll. The news assumes a new doomed shape.
Great Writer, have you put down your pen? Our grief is a cliché to you.

Friends call to say with tourists gone the sea turtles have thronged
our childhood beach. If you were here, this is the joy I would replay for you.

Pyres pock your city. The losses burning day and night.
Fire after fire—it's like my heart is on display for you.

Valmiki found his meter when he cried out in distress.
This poet, daughter, penitent looks for a shape that lets her stay with you.

KIRUN KAPUR

Elegy with Silver Paper and Sweets

Once he drove straight into a mithai shop. None of us were witnesses.
Tumbling metal chairs, the shocked vendor, silvered burfi scattered
on the windshield—all this I have imagined. What did he say about
it? Only that the mishap transpired at the corner of Shankar Road,
that he was driving the old Austin of England. He was laughing as he
told it, his hands mimicking the absurd size of the steering wheel, the
tilt of his head somehow conveying the flush of dust and scrambling
eaters. Certainly, one or two monkeys looked on. His delight that no
one was hurt, that in his telling no one could have been.

KIRUN KAPUR

Elegy with a Honeymoon

He declared to his young bride: he would go water skiing. Dal Lake
glittered, gold and green. She swayed among the lotuses, the painted
house boats, watched sharply bearded men in skull caps speeding by.
He squired her about: Look, the fringe of Himalayan peaks reflected
at the edge. Look at all the jewel-bright floating markets. Each day
was a cool cloth to the forehead after those first married weeks in
Delhi, where 8 am burned hot as their wedding fire. It was a dash-
ing thing to do… To whisk your bride away to paradise, to water
ski bare-chested around a famous lake. A husband: the only person
she knew for days in every direction. A wife: a foreign wonder in
a new pink sari. The pull-boat looked leaky, the tow rope too long
and frayed. The men in charge were laughing, assuring: Nothing
for memsaab to worry about. And he laughed too. It will be fine. No
problem. Like the war that was not a war that she had never heard of.
The war going on beneath the perfect surface of this place. Her pale
face caught the spray as her husband whipped round and round the
lake. It was a full week before she learned that he could not swim.

KIRUN KAPUR

Elegy with an Immigration

In the new house, in the new country, he planted grass. A lawn. Every house in this rich country seemed to have one. It seemed to be the chief conversation of men standing around with drinks at weekend gatherings. In khaki pants, he raked the dirt, he spread the seeds, following the instructions of Steve from the hardware store. How I wish I could remember what he wore on his feet. And within weeks, as promised, one million green filaments shot up, as if he'd spread a carpet of dollars under the oaks. Each morning, he sipped Darjeeling tea and looked out at America. Until the day a doe and her three fawns raised their heads to look back at him, from the only shred of would-be lawn that remained. He cursed, then laughed, then rolled up the sleeves of his pressed white shirt. He said, *I'll re-seed. Otherwise, what else would these fine Americans eat?*

KIRUN KAPUR

After the Appointment, Walking & Searching *John Keats*

Bird or bard, you are
shade of a younger, vaguer self—an ode

      reloading, connection slow
      or you are a shadow

of my current fear—ghost of, gloss on
the screen in my gloved hand?

      Will you come to the river where I stand
      —buffering—buffering— scrolling—

colored plastic bright around my feet?
Speak, please, as plain as trash or text—

      I haven't learned to summon much,
      though I've had more years than you

and when I call up every word
you wrote on this bright star in my hand,

      I make your birdsong with my lips.
      Under the willow stripped of leaves but holding

an oriole's empty nest, I wonder over
 what you've left—what's left

      is grey as a ghost's mouth
      with a single orange feather

suspended from the rim.
Look, Google has informed me

      no nightingales live here— Darkling,
      don't carry me into eternal realms,

don't show me how to make
a bird-faced icon or Top Ten list

       (45 is the new 25, they say). Immortality
       is not my habitat. I need the craft

of its opposite—the natural and unnatural
years and months when you lived

       but knew— show me what to do.
       Show me how to write an end.

ANNE ELEZABETH PLUTO

Texas Tumbleweeds

God knows
how they begin or where they end
as they speed, gather
the lonesome prairie the longhorn
cattle or the sale barn where the culled animals
wait in chutes and are brought out
for bidding before slaughter – it's been
a very long road – and all of your horses
have turned to soul saddle letting go of
bridle blanket just puppet bones of hair and
teeth, of God and memory – oh they carry
love as a specter – their love they carry -
they ride it forever.

MARY BUCHINGER

The Cold and I

In my pocket
the softest stone
   by *soft* I mean
smooth, caressable
I love its cold weight

What is it that moves
between us as my hand
turns less warm
and the stone less cold
What does anyone own?

Cold inhabits
and migrates
   the meteorologist
can track its
trajectory, point
to where it
traveled from—

   a mappable thing
like my life which moves
from room to room
year to year
   someone could say
yes, she was here
on this day
at this hour
I saw her here
she came from there

The cold and I
we sleep
on opposite sides
of the bed
   siblings in the world
of our keeping

More than
a measuring
it's a mingling
   one in the other
and ever so, till I
am all and only cold

CHARLES O. HARTMAN

The Man on the Sad Train

When he cries out we all tighten away.
He's male, young, large, Black like half of us here.

When he cries out so abruptly, he looks surprised.
It sounds like grief. We don't look.

It sounds like grief
no one could contain. It clambers out of him

all claws and panic, and vanishes among us.
A stop later it comes again. He's moved

across the car. After the second stop
he begins to sing softly—high, sweet, unsteady,

perhaps a hymn. At Thirtieth
he carries his bent life off

and the cry stays on,
invisible. The letters

on the station wall strain at their border. The tiles'
grout weeps.

Half of us are male, too.
Among us is one silence.

CHARLES O. HARTMAN

Mindsides

Now and then my masseuse
does something on one side that makes me think

how good it's going to feel
on the other: in the feeling,

and out of it, at once,
all in same brain—how daft is that!

It's like marcescence: how the oak's
dead leaves stick with the oak,

maybe to make browsing noisy and browsers nervous
or delay leaf rot till spring most calls for mulch

or hold onto water as snow until ditto.
Just so,

the brain-trace of a touch may hang around
to inform the next generation

of sensations. It's a theory
for how my weekend time with you

informs the hours in my lonely bed
back at what I yet call home. If it also

explains how stuff done at two
controls the shape of who we are

at seventy-two, the time explanations take
is the time of our lives.

JOSÉ EDMUNDO OCAMPO REYES

My Language

The moment I was born, I inherited my language.
In the land where I was born, I fled my language.

The *Doctrina Christiana* instructing us how we should pray:
the colonizer's tongue shotgun-wed my language.

In first grade, I handed in the mimeographed test, blank
save for my name. Try as I might, I could not read my language.

Plosives, nasals, short vowels leapt off my classmates' tongues.
Dragged away by the currents, I grew to dread my language.

MS Word metamorphosed *Mahal kita* into a *Mahler kite.*
On the white screen it bled, my language.

They ask me, *How did you learn to speak English so well?*
An aging snake, each day I shed my language.

José, paano mo ipagkakaloob ang iyong tinalikuran?
Who will speak for me when I am dead? My language.

ANNA V. Q. ROSS

All my poems used to end in sky

but now they end in sleep,
so when you say that sometimes being
with me is like being with a bomb,
a small bomb, you amend,
and I suggest *a grenade?*
as we sit looking at the lake
where the fish make their small,
swift circles as they rise to feed
on all the winged insects emerging
at sunset. And I imagine hurling
myself out there to arc safe
below the surface into the clasping
leaves and muck of pondweed,
moss, and silted clay,
spinning blindly in my churn,
my seconds ticking off in bone,
blood, sinew until a final spasm
and spout splashes me out
to atmosphere, concussing every ear
with my concluding shout.
It's hard to love a bomb.
Maybe this is why at night
you hold me gingerly,
your hand light as a water strider
tracing the pin of my hip
as I release to sleep.

VIDYAN RAVINTHIRAN

My face

in the coffin-shaped hotel mirror
disquiets me now
we've returned from the temple
where my mother knelt and prayed and rose
so many times, circling
the crow-wild building
while faces dark as ours looked on.

"Everything," she said, to reassure
this painted face in the mirror,
"will happen to you."

(The priest's thumb
anointed my brow
with thiruneeru and sandalwood.)

A horse with an overt penis
leaped from the load-bearing pillar
of that Kali kovil with Kalis everywhere:
her paunch bulbous, teeth fangs;
morphed to a sinuous dancing girl;
bent backwards on reversed hands and feet, scuttling
along the ceiling like a Klein-blue spider . . .

(Unless I tell you otherwise
I am always tearing with my nail
at the skin of my keratinized thumb, leaving
panels of woebegone cerise.)

My grandfather's gravestone
is lost. "Everything is gone,
but he was never there. Tomorrow
you will find him in his Sivan temple."

VIDYAN RAVINTHIRAN

Research

The lawn's frozen-over snow
gleams evilly, like polystyrene.
A foot plunged in it to the knee
might as well
have been cancelled from existence,
dissolved into aching particles. As if
that aspect of the universe that has evolved,
in the form of my person,
to the point of wondering at itself
collapsed back into the void that is Brahman.

"I don my mask before exiting the car"
—no longer merely
an MFA-ish first sentence…
Every piece of large, bluish grit on the platform
deserves a platform. Has its shadow. You too
should read Tamara Fernando's essay
on the pearl-fisheries of Mannar.
What wás a paar?
I ask myself that question every day. Sunday
was like summer

—a Sri Lankan summer—
something isn't right. "Sometimes
oysters settled amidst seagrass
[…]
they seemed to live
happily alongside starfish and turtles;
at other times the latter swallowed up
the entire bed." You wouldn't believe
through the window
these brumal golden climes.

(What Orwell said
about prose
is always on my mind.) The mask needs adjusting.
Blood sprang
from diverse nostrils. Divers'. There
is something in my shoe.
Every step reminds me. A particle
whose etiology I could explore, in another article
—no more. Is it you, walking a mile?
I wish you'd stop.

VIDYAN RAVINTHIRAN

Jaffna, January 15, 2023

From the shop-shack—years ago—
at the Kanniya hot wells
I purchased a soft dark hat, my father vetoing the camo-pattern.
Trees entwined, rough bark and smooth.

Disrobing, our driver
sauntered through the glittering crowd
of Hindus and Muslims and Christians,
past a child doused by its parents

with the healing volcanic water,
shampooed, even
—occupying a space
between a woman in hijab and a priest's soaked soutane.

*

Water cannon at Jaffna—no *s*, in my English—
Tamils pulled out bottles of shampoo,
washing the regime
right out of their hair.

*

A soldier yelled "ticket".
Ananthan—it means *the smiling one*—
rebuttoned his damp shirt. Drily
my father emptied his pockets;
but the man with the rifle
meant only,
did we want to enter the raffle…?

*

Nobel, says the OED—meaning Abel,
Clarke, whose Lord Amherst refused
to kowtow; who lost
to the sea and pirates his specimens of honeysuckle?

"Had I not seen several China merchants
shampooed before me, I should have
been apprehensive . . ."
—From the Hindi, *čāmpo:* to press.

VIDYAN RAVINTHIRAN

The Star of India

blanked by unending rivers
of foot-traffic

traipising from diorama to dinosaur
between vivarium and gift shop

—misnamed. A billion or two
years in the mineral depths

of our teardrop
island (they weren't spent

waiting on J.P. Morgan)
moved to radiant union

its milky tendrils
like the dendrites of a neuron.

O
blue-grey cabochon

the colour of my dead
grandmother's cataract!

ELIZABETH A.I. POWELL

Fallow Field

Plowed and harrowed, it lays
in repose, an odalisque or virgin,
the field waits like a constellation
of fireflies arresting time
by illuminating the night.
I alone am responsible
for letting it be. To be left unsown
is to believe the field is not a corpse,
bled to death on a kitchen table:
the till a dilation rod, the burning
a curettage. The rain comes,
a liquid prayer, the field
my endometrium. My womb a vase
that once held a human heart
blooming like a rose. The dried leaves
piled up like lost love's undelivered letters.
My toes inch worm the dirt,
the wind suction is my intuition,
and aspirates seeds and cells into the air.
I am beyond fallow or fertilization. Too late
to stop now. I thought I was
the field, now I think I am the sky.

ELIZABETH A.I. POWELL

Appointment with Cloud

I wait for the cloud
at the appointed time and place,
my cloud has given me coordinates.

I lean against a wall
bleached and unpainted
and look toward the sky.

When it rains like this
I become the humidity
holding the scent of beachgrass,
noticing how moments
are fishes, hard to catch.

My cloud arrives to tell me
not to forget where I come from,
to learn the respect
my mother tried to teach me

I had been waiting
for something grander
more complicated like
the four errors of Nietzsche

but once life finds your
lesson, it teaches it
over and over, until
it's simple. And so

the afternoon ran
toward me like wild
island mustangs, and
doves and church bells
sleeping inside my lies

I had hope for more
direction but my past
or future self didn't send
the right questions
or at least the ones
I wanted answered
that morning.

DEBORAH GORLIN

Dressed

I think about what I'll wear.
How thirty years after the war he fought in,
we buried my father, as he wished, stitched

into his captain's uniform, jacket slit in the back
to fit, shod in discount cowboy boots, along
with a pack of cigarettes, tucked into the pocket.

How the famed Bronze Age Egtved teen, found
nestled in a hollowed oak tree coffin, left behind
fabulous effects, a kicky miniskirt fashioned

from twisted rope, cropped top and belt buckled
with a big brass disc, the outfit purportedly a dance
costume for her worship of the sun god. How,

in India, nothing blackly or whitely Victorian there,
when the wedding gown doubled as shroud,
but the corpse is wound in bolts of silk, exuberant

with pattern, colored mango, turmeric, mustard,
scarlet, with extra cloth to spare, to feed well
the flames, mime the fire pyres. My point

is this: before your death, make your wishes
known. Casket, closed or open, this fast
fashion will be your last remaining body

suit, final flowerpot, that will recall
your exterior, describe the dips and curves,
encase your own harrowing form,

(think Turin, the impression Christ made)
the dwindling outline, before the clothes
deflate like a balloon, scrawny scarecrow,

emptied of your traces. Marvel at the five-inch
high Louboutin stilettos Aretha wore,
changing into five different outfits at her wake,

the queen of soul to the end, shoes vaunting
her arches, lofting her like a human cathedral,
and while her feet seeped

from those sculptural molds in no time,
it was not before she strutted up to Death,
got in his face, insistent he pay his last respects.

RON SLATE

Body and Soul

The soul itself is odorless but can detect over long distances
the body scent of the person it had once longed to enspirit.

Why have I believed that the souls of the dead are too restless to relax?
When they relent, it's peaceful here on the patio.

Although the soul may survive the destruction of the body in a roller coaster
catastrophe, it will continue to loop the loop for some time.

It may soon be possible for the soul to trade one body for another one and
not have to wait for death in order to move on.

A new widow murmured in her sleep — *cats have old souls that were spectators at
the burning of heretics.*

Some say the soul of a heretic is blistered, but to believe such a thing is
heretical since the soul is nothing like the charred body it abandoned.

But of course, if a sorceress causes a person to appear as a goat, their
humbled soul has no choice but to acquiesce.

There is the soulful thought and there is the pulpy brain and between them
there is an E-Z Pass toll plaza. But the miles mount up.

And when a person appears as a goat, they did not "turn into" a goat
at all, no, their body got swapped out for a goat's.

Some people say aliens liberated them from their bodies only to make
their souls feel even more encumbered in other galaxies.

There are souls that would starkly reveal themselves if not
for the avidity of bodies craving celebrity.

Cole Porter sang, "I'm yours for the taking, I'd gladly surrender body
and soul." Imagine such relinquishing, and for what purpose.

The body and the soul wake in the same bed but seemingly
on different sides of town. Breakfast begins the daily détente.

SARAH GIRAGOSIAN

Hideout Pantoum

Where to go when the earth's no cover,
wonder the creatures who cannot match
their fur to season, who can no longer hide
their white hides or feathers in snow cover.

With what language do we grieve a mismatched
body? Once upon a time, the willow grouse rhymed
with snowscape and birch-fretted forest, but what cover
can she fly to now? And the snowshoe hares? Stand-

still bulls-eyes to raptors who pinpoint their off-rhyme
bodies in the overwarmed understory. Out of sync
too are the weasels whose winter bodies stand
in wait too long for the first snowfall, whose bodies

once welcomed snow as a consolation of color. Sync
your clocks to the music of a shattering globe, friends;
this mutiny of climate is ours, too. Remember in your bodies
how it felt the first time a friend spilled all your secrets.

SARAH GIRAGOSIAN

Firestarter

Mother, if I were you, I'd have known
how to jumpstart your heart
and seed miracles in your hair,

how to revive the beautiful wreck of you.
But in the end, hypotheticals are just the future's
promised curses. Same goes for the mothers-

in-waiting that never existed, the tether
of catastrophe that failed to tie me
to family. Grief beaked me in the eyes,

but there are days I see your face
in a bighearted peony or in the new igniter
inside of me, sticky with over-handling.

They say the astronauts in the International Space
Station see several orbital sunrises a day. I'm training
my mind to see the verb of you in your absence:

the gale of the hawk swooping below;
the craze of the mouse's music box-heart;
the grace of your making when you help me avert

small crises. Mother, I miss you still.
Do I become like the soft glow
in Sargent's painting of the Chinese paper lanterns

lit by girls englobed in lilies, carnations, rose?
Do I choke down this fire on my tongue
so I don't catch it on the striker of the world?

Untitled 3

JOSEPH FRASER

After Which

Berries know nothing
of flavor, the ecstasy
 of purplish-blue flesh.
How delicious to not know,
to bite, recline—forget.

Interview With Visual Artist, Ann-Marie Brown

In this issue of *Lily Poetry Review*, I am thrilled to introduce to our readers the renowned Canadian artist, Ann-Marie Brown. She studied in Europe and received a Cultural studies degree from Trent University in Canada. Thereafter she has practiced the challenging and striking media of encaustic and oil painting for many years out of her studio in coastal British Columbia. She has also attended numerous residencies, most recently at the Artsu Studio in Helsinki, Finland.

Ann-Marie's work has been exhibited internationally, and her paintings are held in private, corporate, and public collections around the world, including the Museum of Encaustic Art in Santa Fe and the Women's Art Museum of Canada. Her paintings have been reproduced in distinguished journals including *Litro Magazine*, *North American Review*, *The Guardian*, and *Crannog Magazine*. A short documentary about her work and process recently aired nationally in Canada on the show *Artist in the House*. To see more of her work, go to https://www.instagram.com/annmariebrown.art/

Please enjoy the below Q&A with Ann-Marie Brown, and her eight masterful works published in the pages to follow.

Q: Thank you, Ann-Marie, for taking the time to discuss your exquisite artwork in the fascinating media of encaustic (beeswax) and oil painting. To begin, what drives you to paint, and what drew you to the encaustic medium?

A: I was drawn to encaustic for its sculptural quality. Also, because the process can't be fully controlled. You can have a plan for a painting, but the unpredictability of the process disrupts intention and opens a dialogue with the emerging image. This provides an opportunity for the active painting mind to push the work to a place that wasn't consciously available.

Q: Were/are you inspired by any particular artists, past and/or present?

A: Too many to count. I've had the great good fortune to live for a while in Paris, and while there, haunted the Louvre and the

Musée d'Orsay. Each day, there would be a different work that spoke through the years to me in that moment.

Q: One of the things I admire most about your paintings is the singular finish you create with the encaustic application – almost like an inner glow, an ethereal feel with texture and depth. Without giving away any trade secrets, can you tell us how you achieve those attributes?

A: Quality pigments combined with the beeswax create that glow when the painting is built up, layer by layer.

Q: Does heating wax onto oil paints cause the oils to dry more quickly?

A: Yes.

Q: Have you explored painting on different surfaces? Which do you prefer and why?

A: I have worked on wood panel and paper as well as canvas, but my favorite substrate is canvas.

Q: In this issue, we are showcasing your paintings of the human figure/portraits. Can you tell us about one of your favorites and why it appeals to you?

A: *Desi in Her Mother's Dress* is one that I really love—possibly because she's the one that got away. Galerie d'Avignon in Montreal had just hung the paintings for my solo show, when thieves broke in and stole three, large works, including *Desi*.

Q: How difficult is revision with encaustic and oil painting?

A: Very difficult!

Q: Do finished encaustic and oil paintings require any special and/or periodic care?

A: If the wax is very thick, it can develop a bloom that requires heat treatment to treat. I have learned to use very thin layers of wax though, so this isn't necessary. The paintings shouldn't be hung in direct sunlight or over a fireplace, but really the medium is archival (the frescos in Pompei were painted in encaustic, and they're still bright).

Q: Have you ever collaborated with others? If so, can you describe a
couple of those projects?

A: I'm collaborating right now, doing a project with perfumer
Rohanna Goodwin-Smith. She made me six numbered vials of
perfume. I open and inhale over the course of a few hours, finding
the colors that correspond to the top, middle, and base notes,
and then paint a painting using that palette. When the painting's
resolved, she tells me what the oils were that she used.

Q: We'd love to hear about your studio environment and any rituals
or routines you may have to prepare for a day of painting.

A: I hike in the forest to clear my head and sharpen my senses, then
take a coffee down to my studio and begin.

Q: Do you have any tips for artists who would like to try encaustic
and oil painting?

A: Save yourself!

Q: Lastly, what message do you hope your art conveys to the world?

A: There isn't a singular message I'm trying to convey. I would
say that I hope each of my paintings becomes an experience for
the viewer.

In Her Garden After the Storm

My Haystacks

Texture of Our Loss

ANN-MARIE BROWN **The Storm**

119

ALEX MAYER

I Lost It at the Movies

for Pauline Kael

Fine, I'll admit it: I hated *8 ½*.
O santo cielo! O sacre bleu!
O don't make that face at me!
This is *my* poem, not a film class,
which means I don't have to defend
my tastes, be they turnipy
or otherwise. But O
how I love to make my case.
It's the sin I just can't quit!
Forgive me, Father,
for now I must appeal to the authority
of my lord and savior, Pauline Kael,
who was as right in the '60s as she is in the '20s,
writing that Guido

        has soaked up those movie versions
        of an artist's life, in which
        in the midst of a carnival or ball
        the hero receives inspiration
        and dashes away to transmute life
        into art. "What's the film about?
        What's on your mind this time?"
        asks Guido's wife.

Answer: dick-lust and death-drive.
What else would it be? *Mommy, I'm afraid
of my desires!* God, men exhaust me.
Recently, the man I thought I might marry
informed me that my manner of speaking
was well past bearing.
I wanted to make a case for myself,
but I had nothing to say. I'd heard it before
though coming from him, it hurt like a bitch.

Seven quick words and he ripped
the happy home movie of our future
out of my mind. The screen hung blankly,
like a curtain. I wondered: what's behind?
Dorothy, no! shouts my hindsight,
You won't like what you find! Not a con-man
pulling at levers, but the disordered
neuroses of my mind caged up
like circus animals. It's a disaster!
The seals are sharp with hunger
and the lions furious for the sun.
Each day, the elephant that is my temper
stampedes into the crowd.
In true Fellini fashion, I've exchanged
one spectacle for another.
But the beauty of a poem is,
I don't have to spend a sum
the size of *Cleopatra*
if I want to pitch a circus tent.
Save the cost of pen and paper,
I can try it out for free.
O God, there's so much I want to say
but I'm afraid it's too late. Please, God,
don't accept me as I am. I mean it.
Let me be more than this ragged mouth.

ALEX MAYER

Nickel Madness

October I come into the world blindered
as a horse. A cry of violin

that shocks the swampland, its industries
of citrus, that rude,

rank spirit of America. In a neurotic distortion
of facts, I cast

Louis B. Mayer as my ancestor. I graft my Iberian
rose to his

Siberian pine, letting father get mixed up
with God, his portrait

rolled up like a scroll on the door
I kiss every time

I come home. Sense is an entrance
to imagination —

the dull thud of a nickel in the hand and feet clamoring up
the glass stairs, lights gone down

for the image of a lion's mouth snarling out
a tiger's roar.

What I want to know is: when the storm blows in
from Paradise, how does it *smell?*

That's not important,
grandfather Louis says, laying a fox

around my neck, the clasp inserted
into its quiet mouth.

Due to the good fortune of my birth,
I have a part to play in his America.

I can be sexual and valueless or sexless
and valuable or, later,

a Hawksian broad in well-cut,
sporty styles. Then I'll be loved by the good women,

the honorable men and the saintly mothers all peeping sensation
at the cineplex.

Now you're getting it, he says,
patting my head. Now we're at the door

to his office. It's so big you could put wings
on it and fly it, like a jet.

On his desk, a white phone is ringing.
It's David, with *Birth of a Nation*.

Grandfather answers & the doorknobs turn
to gold.

On his desk, a white phone is ringing.
It's David with *Gone with the Wind*.

Grandfather answers & the windows turn
to diamond.

On his desk, a white phone is ringing.
It's Albert and Harry, with *You Only Live Twice*.

Grandfather answers & the pen fills up
with blood.

Now I'm a child.
I sit on his lap and dip my pinky

in the heavy crystal of his glass
for a taste of whiskey.

This charms the gathered old men.
There's Zukor,

the killer, Harry off Poverty Row
and Carl, called the whitest man in the industry,

which the industry insists
is a compliment, all filling the room up

with smoke —
Cuban cigars and imperial cologne —

They're laughing and listening
to my grandfather extol

how being born and reborn on the 4th of July,
it's made him whole.

MYRONN HARDY

Newspaper Poet: New York City

The Yemeni man in the Yemeni
cigar shop doesn't know you're

a poet. Most of the time
you don't either   all mysterious.

But today your poem
is in the newspaper. There

is one copy left in the shop
where you often buy peppermint

gum or almonds. You attempt Arabic
with the owner who asks if you're

from Yemen. You open the page
where your poem is printed.

Your finger is an arrow through
its aorta. *Yours*   he asks.

You're quickly in love
with that word as he recalls

strangled poets dangling
from dragon's blood trees.

The bells they were
without sound.

LLOYD SCHWARTZ

Corona Blues

*

Eavan Boland, "Quarantine"

I.

It's the night before shutdown, and we're determined to do something heroic.

What were we afraid of?

After all our years together, we decide to get married.

*

First thing in the morning we call City Hall.

We're told to go to the Court House.

It's raining.

The traffic is heavy.

And there's already a line.

When we're finally at the counter, the clerk tells us we'd been misinformed.

We have to apply for our license at City Hall.

On the other side of town.

In the heavy traffic.

In the heavy rain.

At City Hall, we get on another line to get the application we need to get approved at the Court House to get our license at City Hall.

And City Hall, the security guard reminds us, will be closing at noon.

Indefinitely.

*

Back at the Court House, we find two lines.

DIVORCE and PATERNITY.

A guard tells us to pick the line that's shorter.

DIVORCE is shorter than PATERNITY.

The lady at the counter seems happy to see a couple who aren't miserable yet.

She tells us we need to see a judge.

*

In the empty courtroom, the bailiff yells at us to stop whispering.

The judge is nice—she asks us to swear we are who we are and she believes us.

She explains to us the waiting period.

It would be easier to wait.

But we can't wait.

*

The rain keeps getting harder.

Back at City Hall, we need to find a Justice of the Peace.

But the ones who work there are all engaged.

On a list they give us, you find a dimly familiar name.

You like her name.

You phone—and she answers!

"Come on over!" she tells us.

She works right across the street.

She's married people before—and she's good at it.

Her officemates are enthusiastic witnesses.

Everyone's happy.

Then she reminds us we still need to get our license.

She grabs her raincoat, says "Come on!"—and races with us back to City Hall.

She sails into the office: "Hi, girls!"

"Hi, Denise!" they call back.

"Stop everything! These nice folks need a license."

But the printer's down.

"Get Jack!" someone yells.

It's almost noon.

Then Jack appears and slams the printer hard enough to print out our license.

The office quietly returns to its shutdown, and we, with barely a minute to spare—we seem to be married.

II.

We used to eat out every night.

Every night!

I'd ache for a home-cooked meal.

Now home is the only safe place to eat.

So we order our dinners delivered from the same places where we ate out.

But our favorite places are closing.

We have to cook—which is often a source of tension.

Increasingly often.

*

We must avoid the danger zones.

Each of us fearing for the other's safety.

"Bread for days on end drives all real thought from my brain."

*

One morning a neighbor tells me she saw someone talking to their cat.

"I told my dog," she says, "and we both laughed!"

*

It's increasingly hard to concentrate.

I want to be productive, but nothing works.

Nothing new.

I look at things I abandoned.

I worked hard on them.

But I don't know how to fix them.

*

We watch the news, until we can't stand any more.

Then murder mysteries—for the happy endings.

And old movies.

In a Lonely Place, From Here to Eternity, Night of the Living Dead.

"Every disaster movie," someone says on TV, "begins with ignoring a scientist."

Duck Soup.

*

A friend sends us a link to a video—old dancing stars synced to a funk soundtrack—kicking up their heels with such lightness of being!

We watch it over and over—we never want it to end.

*

You get an email from an old friend:

> *Dad was doing fine, determined to live to 100. On his birthday we had a big party and he was alert, happy, chatting, and blowing out candles. There was absolutely nothing wrong with him. Then he got the virus. First I blamed the faceless pandemic. Now I think I'll blame the president.*

The Queen addresses "people of all faiths, and of none"—and tells us we're

> *discovering an opportunity to slow down, pause, and reflect in prayer or meditation… We'll be with our friends again. We'll be with our families again. We will meet again.*

A doctor warns people from New Jersey:

> *Stay home, please God, stay home!*

*

The president gets the virus.

A friend leaves a message: *Is the bastard dead yet?*

We hold our breath.

We don't enjoy our *Schadenfreude.*

Then we do.

*

We know we're lucky to be together.

But tempers flare at the slightest misapprehension.

How can anyone bear the isolation of living alone?

Hard enough to bear the isolation of living together.

If we get the virus, we want to get it together.

*

Eventually, there's a break in the weather.

We meet a friend for a stroll in the open air.

A pastoral walk in a beautiful old cemetery.

People we like are buried there.

A few days later, we put a down payment on a plot.

APRIL GIBSON

After reading Ed Roberson's *Asked what has changed* then looking out the window

AND NOW, the 17-year cicada
with a guest appearance from
its 200-year-old kin. Billions.
They descend as predicted
through counties, suburbs,
southern swaths of Lincoln
land, reports of screaming
locusts in flight, exoskeleton
boneyards heaped upon boles.
A Chicago pastoral unfolds
lush canopies curtseying
above scarred bark, thin
tailed squirrels, frantic
and gray leap to the metal
chorus of the braking "L"
Listen for the piercing screech,
the crack, wiggle, then winged
bodies emerging, fly-beetles
crying out, crashing before
falling into sacrificial love.

APRIL GIBSON

Riding the Borealis

I.

A nine hour trip across the Midwest
reminds me how much space is left
in America, and that there is enough
for millions to frolic and grow corn

without Wi-Fi or nearby hospitals:
one emergency sign for every 20
billboards flashing giant fetuses,
browbeating onlookers to keep

what they may or may not have
in their bellies. I hope I do not
get sick on this voyage riding
centuries old rusted tracks

in freight traffic on a train
with a name that's Latin for
heading North. I can only
imagine the Aurora lights

in the dark of night weeks ago.
But today the sky is gray, dull
as the muted green of Amish
girls' plain dresses receding

as their large families file into
rows and the rest of us pretend
not to notice the influx of white
bonnets, ribbons, and straw hats.

Try not to stare. Pay attention.
It's the cafe car lady muffling
over the mic: Finally, time

for hypertension in a bag,
microwaved burgers, mini
bottles of vodka for dessert.

II.

Surveying the other side of the window
that can't decide if its round or square,
we breeze past farms and wooded areas
like a Zephyr heading home, we span
hundreds of miles of what feels like
wide nothingness to folks like me.
So much green that I am quieted,
quite bored then curious why hardly
anyone lives in the middle of it all,
if the world is running out of room.
I recline my coach seat 100 degrees
and stop being obtuse about the truth:

The world's problems are no more
a matter of space than a matter
of money, a point of power
and keeping people out or in,
ruling where, when and if
having a place to call home
is a right, if land is a rightful
possession, or a cause for war,
the price to stay, the debt nature
is always left to pay, the cost
of doing business they say, may
sometimes result in a loss,

                    a waste,
                    a wasteland.

III.

Grateful for the gift of clean water,
for a moment, at least, though I no
longer drink from the tap.

GLORIA MONAGHAN

Dear Father

Happy birthday. Last I heard you died in Juarez,
but that conflicts with the obituary
that states you died in upstate New York—
or in a small apartment in Ann Arbor.
I do not remember
your smile, or blue eyes shadowed
in the darkened hallway where you whispered
your confession into my hair.
You advised me to read Trollope. I did not—
you also said, *do not dog ear your book*,
so I dog ear everything from my bed
to the dishes.

GLORIA MONAGHAN

House of the Vanquished

Dogs bark in the darkness
before the thin line of orange appears—
just above the white water's break along the sand.

In the dream I was married to the same man I divorced. I
was the 1950's wife—
everyone else cut their hydrangeas back before winter.

Driving south, I see a cedar waxwing high in a tree calling to his
mate. Perhaps it is a sign—hollow, haunting, lonely.

The mouse moves in the walls of January—
putting off any decisions of permanent location.

I had let him make all the important decisions and
stuck to my recipes and inventions.

I even collected aprons and wore them nude
until I could no longer ignore the wolf at the door.

GLORIA MONAGHAN

Letter to Violet Paget (a.k.a. Vernon Lee) from George Sand

*The long lean face of a starved horse, and large and intelligent eyes not
wholly devoid of obliquity, revealing a dental display of really deplorable
character, and on her head, my dear boy, from nine to thirteen hairs.*
                        —Henry James' description of Violet Paget

My father sold canaries and finches on Quai Aux Oiseaux.
As for me, the sympathy for birds
is so deeply ingrained that my friends think I'm insane.

Perhaps they played a role in my former lives.
The bird, I insist, is a superior being.
Its flying ability places it above man,
its beak and claws possess unparalleled dexterity; consider
its instincts for conjugal love—
its nest a masterpiece of skill and
scrupulous comfort.

The birdman is the artist—
the dog-man, not a likable type.

In Venice, I lived tete-a tete with a charming starling
which, to my great despair, drowned in a canal;
then I lived with a thrush, one I had to leave
and parted from with pain.

We live in a time in which we cannot explain
the natural causes of miracles.

Listen, my life is yours. You
are a dreamer like me.
You who read me are not immersed in the fracas of today's world—
otherwise, you would push me aside in boredom.

GLORIA MONAGHAN

Letter to George Sand from the 21ˢᵗ Century

Mignonette,
how delighted I was to read and receive your letter,
the one with the fatal stamp of your grandmother's seal, the bleu nuit,
which suits my mood, my endurance, and my idea.

From Braintree, light purple lilacs bloom only at the top of the tree next to
the red bud tree. The azaleas in the side yard just now fall—
and beneath them spread lily of the valley, sought after for bridal bouquets but
invasive and poisonous to cats, a reminder
of all those sad dreams of me with my ex's family.

Their looks of false acceptance and false kindness— and
my fawning attempts to pick up the house.

People don't write letters anymore,
Amantine, they post. Endlessly about a moment.

Remember when you wrote, *Dear scandal lovers,*
close my book now. Remember the charming starling in Venice?
Now, people don't have time for anything
much let alone a tete-a-tete with a bird.

Last night I went to Gloucester to hear poetry.
There was a small house. The air smelled of fish and ocean. You
are my beloved, you are a dream, a composition delicately layered
in my mind, a soft quilt from another time.

You wouldn't like it here. Last night, I remembered my mother paying
for horse-riding lessons; even then the cost was too high for her, but she liked to sit
behind the glass, watch me in my skullcap riding hat
atop a beautiful red mare. Black boots, barn smell, winter air, my mother behind
glass gleaming smile. I was her then, she is me now.

We changed hands atop that horse,
posting, walking to trot—
oh not like you
riding in a forest of trees among the rapeseed and mimosa—

oh not like that, not like when your servant took your silver stirrup
because they were all afraid for you riding at dawn.

Just mother, taking her last 240 dollars to pay a retired jockey to
teach us to canter. Him threatening to kill the horses—
to sell them for dog food if we didn't do it right.

AYAZ MURATOGLU

Separating Circle

The landscape that made itself obstacle was
green and glittering under a thistled sky.
Your hand reached out to me from beneath the bed.

At dawn, a shaking arose from the walls,
stuttering and there. I've only ever wanted more
from the day, its tenor breaking

a hawk with its territory.
If the mosquito bit me
in the middle of the night, and its buzz

made the neighbor tremble, then
clouds aren't tithing after all. Just
claiming it as their own. Prisoner's dilemma.

I check the mailbox for news
turn to see the downstairs dog panting—
no wonder he has anxiety:

he lives with a cop and a yoga teacher
and tho they are lesbians
they trust the state to protect them.

A delicate and desperate time arrives,
your hallelujah barely escaping the space
above your teeth, slipping between—

a timing fails. The clock in the kitchen
stuck a few minutes fast: a future runs
parallel to this one. A nearby stream

trembles beneath the weight of your memory:
this one made the morning
this one the arcades

beating
under the city sun.
You, in your park, staring at birds

on a Saturday. Withdrawing from the day
the lone laborer walks towards bed. In between,
someone sets the table

and attempts to distance himself from the past:
wish images fill the cup. The water bottle on the desk
refuses horizon, and turns instead towards a childhood

memory: cream on the counter, water up the nostril.

ELLA SCHMIDT

Creation Story

I meant to call, but my apartment got smaller,
the music louder, the sex worse. The men are depressed
and I am a sudden event—the body concedes,
an animal that has been shot at before.

You are these pecking heavens, violence
somewhere else, billboards
pandering to the better lives
that still riot in the silence inside us,

and I
I am practicing softness and gentleness
in a hospital room. Watching you write, but feeling
you grope for meaning at the bar.

I step upon your scale,
the station of this longing, the quiet injury of your favor.

I have seen your eyes darken with kindness,
you in California, drawl of crags and desert
and the body's last fighting organs, girls pretty and stupid
pulling plumes of smoke from their lips.

A moon hardens over the state penitentiary,
its movements like the movements of the high arts.
I have no better reason for being
than the eleven-foot smiles of the billboard girls,

I answer to no one, except to common pleasure and
most men, who signify nothing and depend on so much.
You placed this charge in me: I leave them, just God
they bore me with their seeming and needing.

You have cast your dark upon this poem, my critic, you
have made yourself a permanent fixture of language.
Intellectual celebrity, I am an appendage of your early work—
you put me here, I disobey, completing creation.

More plain sparrows, you say, a stillbirth,
some small domestic dispute.
Too much attention paid to women, and women with men.
Too many leggy blondes, bar fights, a motor inn—

when my lips move, reading,
yours move too.

BRAD CRENSHAW

You Know What?

I would, if I were kinder, lie about
my disapproval, or dissemble when
you throw away your little money on

a fantasy. I fake the sage, distinguished
face of silence as your husband leaves
in company, same way as ever,

with a princess flourishing her foxy
diamond belly rings. Synthesis
is tangled. When I say you've rid yourself

of useless crap, I mean you're homeless, I mean,
you're surfing someone's couch these days in Oregon,
and leave with borrowed tanks to dive at sunrise

somewhere off of Orcas Island. I watch
your video of pelicans, and seabirds
early with their whirring wings stealing

bait until you're falling backwards from
the stern, positively buoyant,
and breathing deeply underwater. That

looks easy, but I catch my breath
with you among the eels weaving in
and out of coral beds and sponges. Since

you fed that common octopus by hand,
all I've heard about are plans for your
tattoos. I have no help in judging you,

who savor oysters over lunch, each
twisting in your open mouth, and then
forgo your medicines because you over-

spent your income for the month. You just
go nuts. So now your lower legs
are numb, your retinas will take another

hit from neural plaques. You are harassed.
On any average rainy, thunder-driven
evening, there is no loneliness

like yours, although to give you credit where
it's due, you are mistress of your hours.
Inquire after logic, and your single

women friends appear on instinct like
a suite of deer, all collective vigilance
intact, and take you in together, happily

companionable, over-generous
and, I wonder at times, how affectionate.

TZYNYA PINCHBACK

An Incomplete History of the Endangered

The summer we empty the bird feeders,
I lose my faith. Our upstairs bay windows
stare, nest high, into the yard dense with pines
and a redbud tree that shades two granite
bird baths – dumped, dry and sheathed in dark plastic.
It all began with a novel flu, your
father, in sleep, flown out from his body.
And then the grackles—glossy, black corpses
iridescent in grasses from D.C
to as far west as Ohio—followed
by the blue jays, starlings, and house sparrows.
Just like the roof on that old split-level
off Sandwich Street, we learn isolation
can warp, waterfall around you, a shroud.

TZYNYA PINCHBACK

My mother's Bible is the evening

Fill'd with the praise of him who gives the light …
— Phillis Wheatley, A Hymn to the Evening

shutting its eye on a horizon, vast
and filled with ache. The last stop
on a city bus line without fare or transfer.
A drawstring purse yawning
to reveal a stash of baggies, creased new bills
from the walk-up ATM at the corner of Winston and Wall.
Her pristine cursive dressing the margin,
each translucent page of the Book of Psalms.
My mother's Bible — flanked by oyster shell ring dish,
my daughter, posed in commencement gown
and hood — gathers no dust or shadow,
its spine slack against my bedside table,
the full grain splitting her name
in gold letters glint against the red-brown leather
as if scripted with light.

SARAH LEIDHOLD

After I quit Botox

My ego couldn't afford
those fault lines but
my wallet couldn't
afford the price of poison;
my wallet won out.

Botox is taut control-
it's not letting life write
its poetry on my face.
Erasing all echo of emotions-
destroying the evidence of rage and
ironing out devastation's heavy footprints.
I was desperate to be tabula rasa
when on the inside I'm all watercolor.

Slowly I readmit life's poetry back on my body.
The laugh lines return first, tiptoeing in silently
and then settling in. My forehead is a palm to be read:
this line traces back to the 716 times I threw
my head back, my giggles applause for clever jokes.
This one is etched in pain, and this one is proof
of how heavy it was to carry that worry.

I let softness back in, let messiness show;
my face, an unmade bed, a rough draft.
When I'm angry, let it bring my brows
together and let it be known—she's pissed.

As I listen to my student tell me all about
their imaginary pet fox, I don't pause
to consider the price of adding a line—
I let my eyes widen and feel
the skin fold in the currency
of time and connection.

DANIEL E. PRITCHARD

Forty-One Weeks

Your fetus is the size of a Brazil nut!
the email read. Then it was a grape,
then a kumquat, then a satsuma—
that came after the *ocean of blood*
drew other bloods from your body
like a tide, to quote a helpful nurse.
When you fainted that first time
your eyes blanched like a turnip.
Everyone had something to say.

Can you feel anything? Can I feel?
Will you find out? Well, I can tell.
I can see from how she's carrying.
Nana hung a ring over your belly
like the tarot of the hanged man
to divine the sex. It wouldn't swing.
What about the nausea? you asked.
At twenty weeks, it was a rutabaga
able to hiccup and dream—of peas,

maybe, or of a bird with a snake,
or kettle drums, hostice, or of you.
When the car backfired in traffic
and you fainted again, you dreamt
that you could hear a pair of buttery
heels pounding on our roof.
I began to really see your body,
the shape of it, that it had shape.
It became a ripeness other than itself

all thickened hair and night sweats.
A taproot drove down into you,
through your ribs, hips, and feet,
and when the lightening came
it clutched the soil of your voice

and discovered your damp breath
fogging the mirror morning
and night, clinging to the sink,
hissing at the red and bloated face

you—will not—be sick—you…
And despite an esophageal aversion
to so many smells, you wanted
to cook. Even the sight of meat
made you sick, chicken breast
in particular. We ate cauliflower tacos,
russet potatoes, zucchini, mushrooms.
The nausea would last to the final
push—I held your hand and a bucket.

This brought you further beyond
yourself than ever, on the outside.
Inside, you were a field of likenesses:
calabaza, speckled swan, parador,
delicata whose bloody show
knocked you flat that final time
at the bus stop along a main road.
I cradled your head, blonde hair
pooling on the concrete. I threw

my phone into traffic and screamed.
We hadn't had an email in days,
I didn't know what to call it.
We were well beyond metaphor.
How could we have known, after
images of pea and plumb, that you,
lying on a filthy median, would become
finally, a fig, stretched and darkened
with a wasp inside starving for life.

MARTHA MCCOLLOUGH

The suffering of suffering

I don't have to be anywhere
or speak, though I might—

in this one way
it's good to be old

transient bubble of peace
before the suffering sets in

years rolling downhill
abyss a step away

a child steps along the curb
arms out, wavering

as if on a tightrope
as if a long fall were visible

enjoying imaginary risk—
in the distance war

washes back and forth
over the world

MARTHA MCCOLLOUGH

Notes for my creditors

I hardly think of you.

I hardly think of you as human, and you, you want
to scoop me like a plum out of my skin, with one turn of the spoon.

This is a spell not a message.

Once from Manhattan Bridge I watched a warehouse burn, flames
ascending from the midnight windows toward the rusty van where
I leaned out, amazed to see so much surplus value vanish in that
festive conflagration.

My threadbare morning casts no shadow.

Back then the bridge set down its giant foot among weeds and
broken cobblestones. Stencilled on a ledge the word "decay". Trees of
heaven grew straight out of spalled brick walls. No one expected the
subsequent influx of millionaires.

Someone is knocking. Is it you in your false mustache?

I have composed a catalog of useless things I am allowed—poetry,
etcetera. Think of me sleeping, blissful, earning nothing.

No really, I *have* wasted my life

J.D. SCRIMGEOUR

Savers Thrift Store, Danvers, Mass

Two of the three pairs of jeans don't really fit,
but I get them anyway—only five dollars,
no obvious stains, and they can go to my son,
Aidan, who is skinnier. At the checkout line
with Eileen's 62 children's books, the cashier
trusts us when we tell her the number,
and tells us we basically got the pants for free,
since we get a free book with every four,
and Eileen says the books are all going to her school,
and the cashier says great, says she bought
24 shirts herself, using her employee discount,
and brought them to the shelter. It made my day,
she says, and hands me our receipt…

In one of the books *I* bought, Gore Vidal
talks of how he became a radical:
the text of an interview from his villa in Italy
where he hosted Susan Sarandon—
her kids swam in his pool—and I wonder
if you can be a radical in a villa in Italy.
The other book I got was *Survival in Auschwitz,*
the Polish guard wiping grease from his hand
onto Primo Levi's shirt, mindlessly,
as if Levi himself was a rag.
If This is a Man was the original title.

Let's go back to children's books. How great that Eileen
got a giant *Frog and Toad* book for her classes
so they will actually be able to see the pictures!
We'd read that book to Aidan before he could talk:
how Toad went to get ice cream for Frog,
but the ice cream was melting as he hurried back,
and he tripped and the cones glopped onto his head,
and no one would get to eat anything.
Aidan, hardly more than a baby, listened eagerly,

then, pages before the ice cream melted,
he'd cry and cry. We couldn't soothe him.
And slowly we came to understand
he knew how it would end,
that though he could not speak, he understood.

J.D. SCRIMGEOUR

The Never-Ending Song of the City

for N.V.

You leave the train with such joy
that your dress smiles with flowers,
and Wen, the boy from China
who works sixty hours a week
in the mall's food court,
holds your hand. Was it the day
you began to learn his language,
how to write the ideograph
for friend, that those years
began to slough away?—hunched
in school hallways, K-pop
popping through earbuds,
your Puerto Rican mother's
admonitions—*it's not your culture*—
haunting you just as school
haunted you. Class after class
you wouldn't, couldn't speak,
head tucked into your chest.
They said you needed to do this
to become a success.

That's all at your back now,
a train stop in the past,
and as you nearly skip
past the conductor, you notice
the newly planted blueberry bush
between the platform and canal.
The chemicals poured in the river
before your ancestors came
can't ruin these blueberries,
but you'll have to share them
with the starlings (another immigrant).
Wen is so tall! His head almost as high

as the grand heads of the Chinese Zodiac
on the Rose Kennedy Greenway.
The dragon and snake extend
their tongues to taste the market's
waft of ripe fruit. As you take
the long route through the park to Chinatown,
still holding hands, the foxglove,
roses and poppies raise their fists.

JENNIFER MILITELLO

bone

Through the skull, one can see the dream as if the eyelids were
undone by the body's crawl or by the garden there within. The ghost
still in love with the flesh. The incorrect guess. The stairwell's echo.
The thunder's fuss. Through the ulnar, one can see the torn versions
of the birth, the shaking there in the first moments, the clogged
breath, the day mining its way through the window, clawing like
a crow to get to the new child, the one child warmed by the skin,
the single child who is also many and slips through the world like a
scalpel, leaving a mark, its small lungs inhaling the particles, its small
hands repeating the same motions and then the cry coming right from
the lungs while the bed sheets stitch a whiteness the child will never
remember, the child will never forget. Small hunch at the body of
another. The lantern of the skull untaming light until it flies in the
face of the host, a world outside that aches for that entry and a
separate place. Through the face, one can see the woman where one
was made and the hospital bed retching with this woman's pain.
Through the skull, the day one has dreamed simply by being, and the
giving one forgets to take. The salt of life sifting. An hourglass shake.

With my head in the clouds

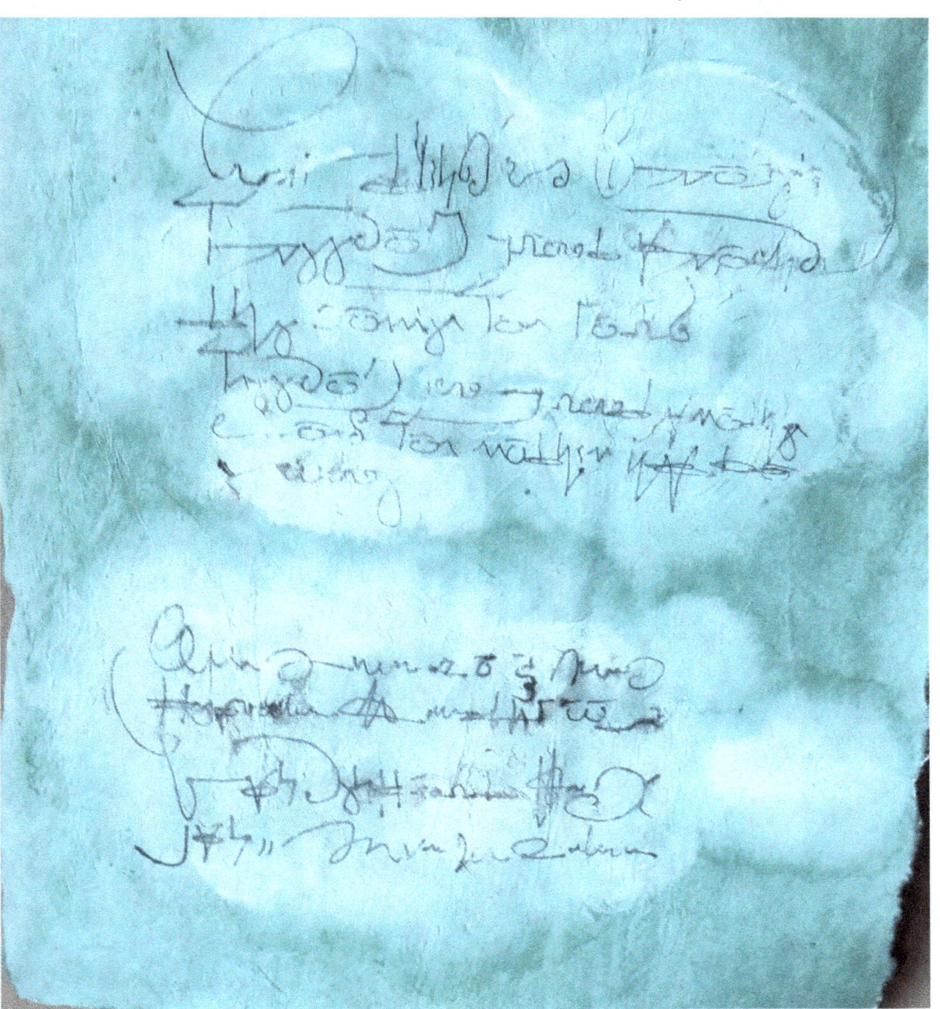

PATTIE MCCARTHY

from books about houses by the sea—

And the big black cormorants go by, flying very low, with necks outstretched, making
that same urgent line across the water as a wild goose against the sky,
and carrying   their absurd courting gifts of scraps of seaweed, tokens
of nests to be.

—Tim Robinson, *Stones of Aran*

you can touch each
side of the house with your hands— nearly

coastal use & reuse   a spindle
juxtalittoral   a quilled ripple   — sea

tangle & girdle— fingered kelp
I mistranslated

the beginning of the tide at full speed as
the beginning of the beach at the end of the day

it is a color I recognize but cannot
place except in this place

this will require some patience
more patience   patience

I'm not sure we
remember how to have

attention is not finite
victory is not finite

colors we recognize change &
arrange as the tide

falls or floods
falls or floods

tides unfold— nest
near estuary with enough

sunken drumlins for every
day of the year—

that the sea might find
me in the dark with

your mouth—
a message that never loses

its urgency—seaweed clenched
the mussel like pulmonary arteries   like pulmonary veins

a ridiculous circuit of thought
takes me past the history of *deer*—

that is or was any animal— any
four legged undomesticated

animal in english to the irish
fiadh— also deer also

once any animal wild & outsized
as once *girl* was any animal

young & obscure in origin & now
tearing through the surf at keel

heavy surf   heavy work
whatever the narrative is of

the coast   up close   it must
be disruptive — a pattern of gulls

abraded   the foreshore stretch left
bare when a wave recedes — a relic —

what I want is relentless
observational desire— long

blank morning reflective trawmore
an uncanny low tide

JUNE DAOWEN LEI

2001

Maybe twenty times before I've written
of the sky so blue that in memory

it felt like play: crayola lego sun
acrylic monoscape of child's paint

or the teletubby world from TV—
iotas of dream, conjuring a day

so ideal, so azure that what happened
next was out of a movie, but not fiction,

not memory: the chasm called to all
the children *heal us, bury us,* wretched

screech and smell of the burning buildings
combusting, acting coy with gravity—

a unclouded world of before, and then the
hazy life that happened in the one afterwards

my girlhood cracked like an egg and spread blue
viscous and useless, slick as cell division

and fermented, as if reverting back
to an earlier version of the draft.

rewind: the tragedy that hadn't happened,
the gauze uncovered the wound

what I remembered was a preamble,
the clouds a distraction

the deal was peace. The price was peace.
The children, they were us too.

MATTHEW E. HENRY

The Most Dangerous Game

After Candice M. Kelsey's poem of the same title.

I have never taught the short story by Richard Connell, but
I have never been able to keep it at more than arm's length.
it seems to pop up every time I turn on the news. especially today

as they play, on repeat, the last moments of the young jogger—
the student at South Georgia Technical College shot near his killers'
Satilla Shores homes. I have been teaching remotely since mid-March.

being home for the last two months has bred the unhealthy habit
of staying informed. I have read it's a tradition for many fathers
and sons in southeastern Georgia to enjoy the outdoors by stalking,

killing an unsuspecting buck. that cellphone recordings are the new
trophy. that there's a straight blue line from "slave patrols" to
the sheriff's office. living outside Boston, the land around my home

is mostly protected. a no-hunting zone you might say. I have never
been killed—at least not yet—because I don't jog. but I have been
followed, pulled over with ill intent. I tell my students the news

about Ahmaud. guilt-ridden soldiers searching for a Brown body—
drowned headfirst in O'Brien's imagined field of mud and shit—
is supposed to be our topic of discussion. months later, a few

will march around their town green acknowledging George's final
nine minutes with a knee on his neck. for now, the white faces behind
nametagged black squares remain mostly silent. traditions are funny things.

they become rituals, like thoughts and prayer, or obsessively checking
the news to see if another who looks like me was shot where she sleeps—
how Breonna's pillows were bloodied the night after covid closed

our classrooms, sent us to the safety of home. traditions can be the stories
we learn, the fictions we teach. like that one about the crazy island where
white men hunt other white men for sport. that stupid author got it all wrong.

MATTHEW E. HENRY

La voix du silence

1928, oil on canvas
René Magritte

here—as with hallways and highways—safety
is more probable if one stays to the right. there
are things which you cannot unsee. focus on
the parlor built for two in shades of sienna,
aloewood and burnt ochre. sink into the blue
loveseat—so empty and inviting. plant yourself
before the painting within the painting. ponder
the indistinct pastoral—the blue-green slope up
and away. question the brown chairs around the table,
white-clothed and waiting to be set. the green fronds
sprouting from the plinth, the tiny family portrait,
the earthenware jar and single plume perched
atop the shelf: reach for these like the light
seeping through the slightly drawn curtain. but stay
here, on the right. do not broach the liminal space.
do not pass the central beam holding the white ceiling
of sky aloft. do not learn what the eye eschews. why
both brains—mammalian, reptilian—recoil from the dark,
reject the shadow encroaching around the threshold.
the terror unimagined. the things which cannot unsee you.

ELLEN MILLER-MACK

Evolution

They want to stay conscious but can't.
As men return from the womb
they drop into a blue milk stupor.
The planet slowly feminizes.

A woman can leave her elemental sadness
in tangled sheets,
get dressed and demand accountability
from the government.

While a man sleeps, a woman should disconnect
faulty wiring.
Someday she'll slip the skeleton key

out from under
his sex-induced slumber
and release political prisoners.

A man wrapped in a woman's fine moist threads
is immobilized, unable to cause trouble.

She can check her calculations
when things are quiet. Or maybe it's just time
to pull on some jeans, pour herself some bourbon
and start peeling onions.

He is unconscious after sex.
She watches leaves absorbing
the late afternoon sun

and dreams of a woman
who will stay inside her
while they plan their trip to Montreal.

ANTHONY WALTON

Daylight Savings

High tide of sunlight
recedes into a night sea of sky
and the chill

silence of four o'clock—

above me a southbound vector
of geese drags winter
into place, a blanket

to enfold summer memory

The leaves have gone
about their business—red-
veined parchment

on which the season inscribes

the wisdom of the year
and I pull my coat tighter
as a neighbor's dog barks—

Something new, this fear of early dark

VIRGINIA KONCHAN

Therapon

I'm a part of your story, you're a part of my story:
an endless bleed. My name a receipt for a purchase
on layaway uttered by people who don't love me,
rather the way I make them feel certain they need.
We're becoming machines, not only with labor but
cellularly: electromagnetic radiation and data feeds
polluting and rewriting our genetic histories until we
morph into automatons so hyperreal no one can even
tell the difference, not that there's anyone left outside.
I, a symptom of the age. I, walking human capital, still
capable of worship and grief, of phantasmagoric reverie.
I grew up in a suburban bubble fantasy hellscape where
everyone was a homecoming king or queen and spent a
fortune on real estate. My parents, who didn't care about
acquiring money nor manicured lawns, were reported by
neighbors and fined for not having a garage after the old
one crumbled, then again for having a loose dog, a mutt
my dad named Meatball that my sister foisted on them.
Can one not know one is being used? If this is a library,
where's the fire, what is the twisted logic behind cultural
acceleration and expansion or is it an infectious disease?
When the day takes the day away, where are we to rest,
hide, breathe? How can I bear a continuation of the same
plots and themes, without a change in tempo or intensity?
The devil doesn't want me to get to where I'm destined
to be: savage chaos precludes boundaries, rituals, truth.
I became one with my couch today and thought of you.
This is me trying not to be a dick. What I actually want
is for the dead to return, but my beloveds bade farewell.
I want an encounter, not a spectacle: want to be the hour
thought stops and power rises, a Shekinah revelation of
a dream made tolerable by innovational pharmaceuticals,
lounging with my cat, and biting on leather amid screams.

VIRGINIA KONCHAN

Ex-Voto

After the light Blake calls experience,
after the day's attrition, after acrid heat,
after yet another lonely, unbillable hour
comes the rough scrim of evening tide.
I have no more opinions about it than
a tree would have about its expansion
by a ring: no more regrets than I have
about the passing of the vainglorious
past, a non-event I didn't see coming.
O cocaine, won't you tell me, when
I wake and only my dream remains
who I am, sheared of my golden mane?
I want what dulls pain receptors in the
brain, or blocks nerves from sending
the signals of pain: a modest request,
like beauty, a pleasing centerpiece
distracting guests from their food.
Is to be iterative to become a brand?
Is there a nuclear manness, to man?
Were it not for the body, there would
be no documentation of time in nature.
I reach for the ibuprofen to palliate the
violence, cruelty, and crises of the age.
I miss you like I miss speech, which is
to say like breathing, my favorite drug,
and not at all. Pleasure is my phantom
limb, my casino win, sinner's prayer:
what I surrendered to fulfil my vows.
Now I'm stitched to this world as if
it was the only world, dispassionately,
waiting for a dopamine surge to ignite.
Even nuns need feel-good chemicals.
Don't get me wrong, God: I love not
the metaphorical dark, but the night.

VIRGINIA KONCHAN

Metaphysical

They do not move.
—stage direction at the end of *Waiting for Godot*

The earth is rotating, time flying, and space bending
while I'm taken apart and reassembled in many gazes,
including my own. Historically, the word *want* implies
a lack or deficiency. Do I want for something? Why yes.
Four corners of a mud hut, steady income, a few secure
attachments, water and bread. I have no use for beauty,
which, like real wealth, or want, is hidden from view.
Yesterday, I followed a long, forested driveway, past
private property signs, just to see where it would lead.
A millionaire's compound arose in the mist, a mirage
inhabited by those who have no need of transparency,
nestled away in that deep inaction where music reigns.
Parmenides denied change altogether, believing that in
the way of truth, reality is one, and existence timeless
and uniform. Zeno, also a monist philosopher, agreed,
arguing that that travel over any finite distance can be
neither completed nor begun, so all motion is illusory
when considering time as composed solely of instants.
Centuries later, Henri Bergson introduced a theory of
time and consciousness, *la durée*, in response to Kant
and the pre-Socratic philosophers, after realizing that
the moment someone attempts to measure a moment,
it disappears, as for the individual, time speeds up or
slows down, whereas for science, it remains the same.
Despite the demonstrated observer effect in quantum
theory, emphasizing the participation of subjectivity,
Bergson and Einstein disagreed on the nature of time:
Einstein considering Bergson's views to be that of a
soft psychology, irreconcilable with the quantitative
realities of physics, while Bergson thought Einstein's
theory of time was metaphysics grafted onto science,
one that denied the ineffable, intuitive aspect of time.

I stare into the middle distance at the Greek goddess
of truth, Aletheia, a word that translates as revealing,
disclosure, unconcealment: distinct from veiled Isis,
Moses' veil, and the tabernacle veil, protecting God's
people from his fierce, wrathful fire, until the temple
veil was torn at Jesus' death, signifying his death
and the promise of restoration to God's presence.
The horses of Achilles were Xanthus and Balius:
epic offspring of Zephyrus, god of the west wind,
they were immortal and could speak. I, too, was
fixed to that chariot in war. When Patroclus, who
fed and groomed them, died, they stood beside the
Trojan battlefield together, motionless, and wept.
What is it about grief that turns a heart to stone?
I sit alone, consider stillness: in this immobility
I look, see, and do not desire, for I am content
to think about the end, and of want, being here.
Before apokatastasis, a dramatic complication,
but I'm weary of plot contrivances and scenes.
I want to stop time so that I can live within it—
awaken to a new world, a snow globe shaken.
To run the race, then return to the primordial
garden of existence: naked figures in a dream.

VIRGINIA KONCHAN

Verisimilitude

The cold, the dark, the future—the terror
of the vast unknown shudders my bones.
Dawn breaks. I stand at the promontory
of a home I do not own, at a landscape
grown foreign with winter's embrace:
the rustling leaves, propelled by wind,
trick my eye, espied first as sparrows,
the trees grow more spindly by night.
I am more than halfway through life,
a fact only recently arrived as a fact.
I palm it, the inevitability of a death,
sorrows and regrets that accompany
youth's passing, a touristic souvenir.
Beauty was posited as a capital good;
adjectival clauses, deployed liberally;
banquets could not fail to disappoint
a mind fattened on anticipatory hope.
Lower your expectations, a therapist
once advised: for you and others too.
As if ambition's end were peaceable.
As if the crows in the yard, knowing
nothing of the making of money, the
handling of money, the exchange of
money for goods and services, care
about the manufacture of happiness,
the illusion of destination: they don't.
One finds the remainder of my meal,
cries out to alert its family of harvest,
which is to say of something provided
rather than scavenged: taste of manna
from an otherworldly source that flees.
They bear what I cannot, without pride.
The flock is gone as quickly as it came.
What I've done for a paycheck, my god.
What I've spent it on is scattered abroad
in the bodies of living shadows, memory.

ASKOLD MELNYCZUK

A Mouthful of Air: The Power of Poetry in a Time of War

There's little doubt that Russia's war against Ukraine is one of the best documented in history—we have a profusion of photographs and films, literally millions of posts on social media, along with countless articles in magazines and newspapers, as well as novels and memoirs. Less often acknowledged is the documentary power of one of our oldest technologies, poetry, which has been reflecting on war since at least the days of Homer and the Greek tragedians. But what exactly does poetry contribute to the discourse?

It's commonplace for so-called "people of action" to regard poetry wryly, as a somewhat precious and frivolous activity conducted against the backdrop of the real work being done in the shaping and transforming of the material world by engineers, architects, lawyers, soldiers, and politicians. Poets themselves, on the other hand, have risked hubris in exalting the power of language: "Not marble nor the gilded monuments/Of princes shall outlast this powerful rhyme," writes Shakespeare, scorning the fleeting victories of "wasteful wars" in favor of the lasting triumphs of immortal verse.

Yet poets are surely wise not to over-valorize the role they play during an armed struggle—unless, like Serhiy Zhadan and a number of others, they're also enlisted in the military. It is, after all, nearly impossible to convey the reality of war through language, as Zbigniew Herbert observed in his poem, *Episode in a Library:*

> A blonde girl is bent over a poem. With a pencil sharp as a lancet she transfers the words to a blank page and changes them into strokes, accents, caesuras. The lament of a fallen poet now looks like a salamander eaten away by ants.
>
> When we carried him away under machine-gun fire, I believed that his still warm body would be resurrected in the word. Now as I watch the death of the words, I know there is no limit to decay. All that will be left after us in the black earth will be scattered syllables. Accents over nothingness and dust.

The academy is certainly capable of squeezing the life out of literature.

Fortunately, literature always finds a way of breaking free of its embrace.

We might instinctively imagine war to be inimical to poetry yet it's a strange truth that, for better or worse, war has not only provided writers with a subject, but their direct experience of it has influenced the values espoused in their work. Both Sophocles and Aeschylus were former soldiers who'd taken part in major battles and held high ranks in the Greek military. (Serhiy Zhadan take note: Aeschylus was forty-six when he last fought the Persians in the Battle of Platea). Even the bookish Euripides, who eschewed military service and declared himself a pacifist, made an exception for defensive war, which he regarded as inherently virtuous.

More recently, the first World War gave us T.S. Eliot's "The Wasteland," David Jones' "In Parenthesis" and Pound's "Hugh Selwyn Mauberley" which ends with this damning declaration:

> There died a myriad,
> And of the best, among them,
> For an old bitch gone in the teeth,
> For a botched civilization.
>
> ....
>
> For two gross of broken statues,
> For a few thousand battered books.

The struggle on behalf of that botched civilization continued. Consider the roster of names to emerge from the crucible of World War II—Paul Celan, Eugenio Montale, Primo Levi, Zbigniew Herbert, Rene Char, Wislawa Szymborska, Wasyl Barka, and W.H. Auden.

Obviously, poetry's focus differs from that of journalists, filmmakers, social media influencers, and historians. Poetry centers on "being" rather than "doing," and it's precisely its distance from direct action that defines its singular strength and contribution. In his essay "The Redress of Poetry," the Irish poet Seamus Heaney wrestles with the question of how poetry can be an agent "for proclaiming and correcting injustices" without sacrificing what it owes to the art itself—that is, without becoming propaganda. He points to its capacity to help orient the reader's (or hearer's) inner life while reflecting on the external world. Heaney writes: "if our given experience is a labyrinth, its impassibility can still be countered by the poet's imagining some equivalent of the labyrinth and presenting... us with a vivid experience of it. Such an operation does not intervene in the actual but by offering consciousness a chance to recognize its predicament...it offers a response to reality which has a liberating and verifying effect upon the individual spirit." He further adds that he can see how this might not be enough to satisfy committed activists.

Poetry, in other words, is soul work, offering readers what William Carlos Williams calls "the hunted news": "It is difficult / to get the news from poems / yet men die miserably every day / for lack / of what is found there."

That this kind of work is meaningful for the citizens of Ukraine even during Russia's siege is evident from remarks made at Harvard recently by the writer Yuri Andrukhovych who described the large audiences attending events, from poetry readings to rock concerts, taking place underground, in tunnels and subways, during air raids. "Culture has become a kind of cult," he quipped.

But just what kind of news does poetry offer? What does Williams mean by "the hunted news"? Here we should remember that Williams was a physician, a pediatrician and general practitioner whose work put him in direct contact with people at their most vulnerable. By the "hunted news" he meant that spark of energy he felt when looking into a patient's eyes—when that patient opened to the healing energy of another: that moment when the barrier between self and other dissolves, allowing for a comprehensive and radical recognition of a common humanity and purpose. That such dynamic encounters are more common in times of stress or emergency, when one is ill, or in a war, is worth noting. We've heard many stories about the fortifying experience arising from the collective efforts of communities in crisis. Poetry strives for language capable of communicating such life-affirming energy directly to the reader while offering a shelter, a temporary haven, for all who recognize contemplation and thought as vital, not marginal, pursuits.

I gained another level of understanding of the mood in Odesa, for example, when I read poet Lyudmyla Khersonska: "in a country where everyone's name is fear: / it's a good thing that you don't see a thing / and don't hear a thing. Say to anyone not a thing." The closed society Khersonska described is precisely one in which it's not possible to get the hunted news. In a closed society people are compelled to be guarded, secretive, mistrustful, and for this they pay a price. A closed society short-circuits the dynamic energy exchange which makes life meaningful.

I'd like, finally, to underscore what's singular about the poetry emerging from this war—and to consider what it might say to future historians. Perhaps the most obviously striking difference is that so much "war poetry" has been written by women. "In the Hour of War: Poetry From Ukraine," an essential anthology compiled by two American poets championing Ukrainian literature to an American audience, Carolyn Forche and the native Odesan Ilya Kaminsky, contains work by 12 men and 14 women. The titles of poems alone tell their own tale: "Explosions are the New Normal," "People Carry Explosives Around the City," "In the Hospital Rooms of My Country," "1918," "Sniper," "trees are budding with war," "*eastern europe is a pit of death and decaying plums,*" and "Funeral Services."

In "Take Only What is Most Important" Serhiy Zhadan describes what those fleeing their homes might carry with them, and all they'll lose by leaving: "We will never see our corner store again." It's as though he's trying to prepare himself and his readers for certain inevitable losses, and the hardships to come: "We'll scoop up water with our bare hands, / sit waiting in camps, annoying the dragons of war." Halyna Kruk, on the other hand, emphasizes all the things a person can do without: "how much does a person really need / to reach safety.... / i don't need underwear / don't need a change / except extra socks.... / and it turns out even keys / are non-essential."

Poets remind themselves (and their readers) of the importance of keeping perspective inside the frenzy of war, and move us by displaying a nimble wit under impossible conditions, as in these lines from Iya Kiva: "you get a sickly short haircut / as if preparing your head for something horrible," or in this stanza by Ekaterina Derishava: "you just want to take a warm shower / stretch your legs / sleep the whole night in your bed / instead you lie between sashes / of bathtub and blanket / as if you were a scallop or an oyster / though I be no pearl."

One notices the absence of sentimentality and mawkishness in the poems. On the contrary, consider the rakish wit of Yulia Musakovska's brilliant contemporary allegory, "What's rattling in the bag." The poet re-imagines the story of Cain and Abel in which the older brother slays the younger, then plants one of his bones in the garden from which an apple tree rises. The older brother explains his motivation: "It is because your wife is prettier / your song is louder / your soil is richer, / the apple tree in your garden grows taller. / Give me your wife, / your land, / tie your song / in a knot in your throat." But the dead brother will have his revenge on his murderer: "Your wife will come outside / and take a bite of an apple. / She will fall dead. / Your children will come out, / they will take a bite / and fall lifelessly. / The sun will rise / and burn your house to the ground, / sowing the land with ashes." Musakovska has, incidentally, also written some remarkable love poems during the war, one of which, "The Vow," which imagines an utterly contemporary set of marriage vows, has in fact been used by couples in wedding ceremonies during the war.

In an essay published shortly after the end of the second World War, the Italian Nobel-prize winning poet Salvatore Quasimodo noted: "War alters the moral life of a people. Man, at his return from war, no longer finds measures of certainty in an inner mode of life, a mode he has forgotten or treated ironically during his trials with death....War summons up...a hidden order in the thought of man, a greater grasp of the truth."

I'd like to end by registering the tonal changes evident in two poems by one of Ukraine's great women-of-letters, Marjana Savka. The first, written in 2007 while the poet was on a fellowship in the United States, is titled "Easter Jazz":

> Sonny Rollins
> mad and bearded like a god with his sax
> wild as the wind
> beating against the door
> of Symphony Hall
> prophesizes that spring still has a chance
> to bloom
> and the mindloose jazz
> and my desire
> and blood
> blow recklessly through my veins
> I go
> I dance
> I catch the syncopations,
> Lord of Jazz,
> Bless, please, this our Easter.

The poem is a celebration of a sort of union of secular and spiritual pleasures abundantly available in so-called "normal times." Here the prophet and liberating presence is the "Lord of Jazz" himself, the celebrated saxophonist Sonny Rollins whose music stokes in his audience a desire to get up and dance.

Now compare this with the Savka poem included in the Forche/Kaminsky anthology:

MY GOD SPENDS ALL NIGHT

My god spends all night forming his battalions,
Is a crack shot, wages wars.
My god forgives my curses
As he polishes his stones.
My god won't hide behind my back,
Throws quilted covers over children.
My god buys tourniquets
Then lines up to give blood.
My god can't get a good night's sleep
While the entire country's standing guard
My god allows me never to forgive
And lets me call things as they are.

Calling things as they are has long been one of the poetry's most important functions, and contributions to the general discourse. The poem's note is unmistakably martial. Its tone contrasts sharply to the voice in earlier poem. The innocence of the earlier poetry had been an innocence regained after centuries of struggle. Perhaps the one benefit—because one feels a desperate need to wring something positive out of this waste, "having to construct something upon which to rejoice," as T. S. Eliot put it—the one benefit this new disillusioned voice offers is the gift of disillusionment itself. Because here the poet herself is the prophet faithful to her art's calling by speaking truth to power, by honoring the demands of reality. As another poet, Dmitri Bliznyk, puts it: "Take immortality, God, but give/me this cold apple cellar. Take the souls/and other toys, but let us live."

What will historians make of these documents in the future? Whose version of what happened will they believe?

Remembering is what poetry is good at. Indeed, the techniques of traditional poetry were designed to facilitate memorization: rhyme and meter are mnemonic devices and it's worth noting that, while free verse has long been an accessible mode for Ukrainian poets, many continue to deploy traditional prosody. In one of his most delicate yet tensile poems, the Irish poet William Butler Yeats, addresses the Irish revolutionary and activist Maud Gonne, a woman he once hoped to marry, who is now being publicly attacked by her political enemies. In "He Thinks of Those Who Have Spoken Evil of his Beloved," the poet raises the shield of verse against the banter of pundits: "Half-close your eyelids, loosen your hair, / And dream about the great and their pride; / They have spoken against you everywhere. / Now weigh this song with the great and their pride; / I made it out of a mouthful of air, / Their children's children shall say they have lied."

Today, students all over the world study Yeats' poem. No one remembers the names of Maud Gonne's critics.

This essay was initially presented at a series of public discussions titled "Wartime Documentation: Literature, Memoirs and Testimonies" at the National University of Kyiv-Mohyla Academy, April 22-24, 2024.

DYLAN WELCH

Necessary Angel: *The Selected Shepherd* **by Reginald Shepherd,** Selected & Introduced by Jericho Brown: University of Pittsburgh Press, 2024

"Beauty is insistent; it makes demands. It demands that we see it and acknowledge it, that we acknowledge our seeing, that we be changed by the experience," Reginald Shepherd wrote in an essay entitled "Notes Toward Beauty," which I stumbled upon after reading poems by his mentor, Alvin Feinman, who taught Shepherd at Bennington College before the younger poet earned MFA degrees at Brown University and the Iowa Writers' Workshop, where he read deeply in both literature and philosophy.

Feinman was often overlooked given the complexity of his poetry and the demands it makes of a reader: a difficulty that Harold Bloom associated with Wallace Stevens and Hart Crane. And for much of his life, that was Shepherd's experience as well, although the younger poet also had to negotiate the complexities of being, in his own description, "a Black gay man raised in Bronx housing projects" keenly interested in the literary language of "W. B. Yeats and Wallace Stevens, of T. S. Eliot and Hart Crane," an inheritance he personified as a "necessary angel," one that left him "blessed but also lamed." Shepherd's poems express a desire to be understood as a poet who has full purchase on all aspects and resources of Western literary traditions.

Thus, his poems have aspects of modernist "difficulty" but also loyalty to the full possibility of the lyric, an ethos that was not sync with what he termed the "aesthetic of transparency" popular in the MFA programs of his era or engaged in the politically charged but often inane tics of language poetry. Indeed, there is a prophetic visionary strain of American modernism—from Crane, Stevens, Eliot—in Shepherd's poetry that is *sui generis* and for this reason, among others, his legacy has been obscured.

The Selected Shepherd, edited by Jericho Brown and published in April, presents some of the best work from five collections Shepherd published in his lifetime and secures, definitively if belatedly, his legacy in American letters. In the poems, we find a melding of the personal

lyric with a desire to escape the finite, oppressive, capitalistic world in
the hopes of strengthening a sacred inwardness with himself and his
readers. He often presents a protean lyrical speaker who craves chaos,
is relentlessly playful with form, and engages in self-critique. He pos-
its that reading poetry is an experience in articulating a relationship
between language and experience, and between pleasure and pain:
what Roland Barthes labels *jouissance* – an experience in reading that
breaks down ideologies and approaches a place of "textual bliss."

In Shepherd's poem, "Jouissance," his speaker grapples with a world
that cannot be brought into a coherent order and begins to collapse
on itself:

> I tried
> soldering a scene together out of white, my
> absence, but snow collapsed inside my palms,
>
> left me indented lines and street signs
> someone scribbled over before my time.

The speaker's imagery describes a need for space for his putative Black
identity to flourish within the Western literary tradition, one in which
he finds his "absence." Yet he seeks to unite or "solder" a scene from his
imagination, one that hasn't already been "scribbled over before my
time." The "indented lines and street signs" with which he contends
conjure scholastic and urban worlds that have been pre-inscribed; they
do not accommodate the speaker's linguistic and poetic aspirations.
But he turns to the materiality of his setting, gathering what he can
hold.

>   ... let fingers sink
> in loam leached of moisture, color: a second-story
> window box, one scumbled world (a leaf, a scrap
> of Styrofoam) crumbling between cold fingertips.

In soil symbolically "leached of ...color," Shepherd's speaker gathers
urban detritus that links him to his environs. Shepherd's poems often
suggest that we don't merely see the physical world, but *inhabit* it as we
process our own desires, insecurities, and self-obsession.

His speakers often question if they can ever escape the mirror of them-
selves. In the poem "Paradise," the narrator asks: "when shall I / be

like the swallow, singing the rape / of my voice, but singing past the
rape, something / my own to sing." In extremis, he then calls to a
skylark for guidance: "Skylark, I don't know / if you can find that para-
dise, or lead me to / the blackened ruins of my song." These birds—the
swallow and skylark—register competing elements within Shepherd's
own voice, and suggest repression (a swallowing) as well as freedom and
pleasure (larking in the sky).

The speaker frequently experiences a crisis of faith. Often, he finds that
his survival depends upon a rejection of egoism and old myths. In the
poem "To Be Free," he describes this process and symbolically dresses
himself with royalty and trust:

> Foolish Narcissus frittered himself away
> to a flower, Echo suffered down her life
> to someone else's syllables wind throws
> away. Neither knew how to survive
>
> the period style, long days
> in their disastrous completeness.
> I won't let the myths outlive me, won't drown
> in my nostalgia for the here and now
>
> I lie down in imperial purple
> as if I were the sun, lay my body down
> in distance. Correct all deviations
> and make the moon change its tune.

Attaining such a place of freedom where the speaker's imaginative
capacity can transcend his entropic shifts of self-doubt is most pertinent
and challenging when the speaker writes about his relationship with his
mother and his erotic desire for white men.

In the beginning of "Two Boys Glimpsed in Late Light," the speaker
laments his desire for "the old world / of blue-eyed boys," grappling
with a hunger for intimacy and feelings of shame. Juxtaposing voices,
in which forgiveness and anxiety compete, he eventually comes toward
an acceptance of complex feelings:

> I wouldn't
> want this studious boy to come to any harm; he's not

the one I mean. I wouldn't want to break
these lines in anger. (And the anxious faces of my friends,
all white, all not to blame?)

I'll walk beneath the yellow moon at dusk
and wish for him, I write these lines
for him. (And the broken glass, another skin?)

Within this epiphanic moment, the speaker reassures himself with a clarifying voice, surrendering the poem to his readers to consider how he has arrived at such a place of freedom.

In his oeuvre, Shepherd creates a space for his mother to exist through mask and myth as in the poem "Orpheus Plays the Bronx." In "My Mother Dated Otis Redding," he strips bare the plain facts of her life. And in "How People Disappear," he tests whether metaphor is capable of sustaining the memory of her as she becomes adrift, "lost among the spaces / inside letters, moth light, moth win, / a crumpled poem in place of love." In these poems, metaphor is riddled with doubt that his words will suffice, especially in "For My Mother in Lieu of Mourning":

I've been drowning in my sleep
too long, when will I stop comparing you

Would you have frozen

in these lines? You were their possibility:
now love must find another shape. You left me here
with what you saved me from, and I am equal
to that: absence, wind tangled in a winter tree

defeat dangling from stripped branches
or perhaps it's just a plastic grocery bag

Metaphor fails in the speaker's pursuit, and what he uncovers is a void, a Keatsian space of negative capability where he must surrender and dwell as a subject yearning for love's possibility to take on "another shape."

At the end of his final collection, *Red Clay Weather,* in the poem "My Mother Was No White Dove," the speaker compares his mother to a crow, the night, stars, and streetlights, foraging for a space for her existence within a natural world with which he's been in friction. Yet, in the last three rhythmic lines he qualifies his metaphors to present her as her own *being:*

> My mother always falling
> was never snow, no kind
> of bird, pigeon or crow

Capturing his mother in the act of falling immortalizes her as someone who doesn't descend to the bottom, but stays in our vision like Breughel's Icarus in the course of his fall. Her static vitality enables the speaker to engage with his own survival, cultivating the ability to brave and endure beauty's insistent demands.

HEATHER TRESELER

'A Local Habitation and a Name': On First Books, Last Books, and David Ferry's *Some Things I Said* (2023)

In a first book of poems, the poet constructs a cosmogony, a theory of origin for the universe—both the one that they found in the years of their artistic birth, and the one that was necessary to construct as a condition of survival. Thus, a memorable debut bears the thumbprints of two necessities: what the poet had to say (or assay) in language to know the facts of their imagination and experience, and what the poet posits as a contract between the psyche and its artistic manufacture. Poets build, on the page, habitations in which they can speak what otherwise cannot be readily said (or fully heard) in ordinary discourse.

Yet these houses also have apertures—windows, skylights, front doors, and trap doors—that open to a hidden attic or a root cellar, skyline or power line, sidewalk gossip or melodrama, careening bicycle or stray raccoon. In order to avoid the claustrophobia of lyric, poems allow the reader to see the outdoors but from within a particular interiority. From that inside-gazing-outward, poems can rescue certain profoundly personal truths even when they are, in the journalistic sense, utter fiction. Poems also exercise paradox: allowing for complexities that might otherwise be flattened into wellness platitudes or made to winter in intolerable silence.

Without these traits and without some implicit sense of apostrophe (the address of a specific, if wholly imagined, other or others) the lyric poem risks superfluity and unearned priestliness. It exists as a temporary monument to one's cleverness and will. But the irony has no tenderness, the snippet of song no score. The poem is as ephemeral as a highway billboard or a pop song's autotune: we pass by it, and it produces not more than a synaptic flicker. We do not return, for there is nothing to puzzle or savor.

And yet, when the poet pulls off a successful debut, they must then put it all aside and make it new, *again*: construct another world, offering fresh precincts of concern, different angles of approach, upended assumptions. If the poet is fortunate, they repeat some version of this mildly harrowing process for every book, giving each its own architecture, allowing its materials to dictate its form.

But what about the book that the poet reckons could be the last? Is it time, then, for final summations and pyrotechnic displays, the poet offering a wink and handstand to the juror-critics sitting in the second row, knitting their sweaters? Facing the encroachments of advancing age, serious illness, or debility, the poet marshals their powers, hoping to win a modest bet with time: that the book will be finished before its writer. Indeed, in some cases, a poet's late poems evince startling growth, heightened complexity, and unexpected turns. If great poets evolve not only from book to book but even from poem to poem, each a "stepping stone," to use Seamus Heaney's term, across the murky pond of self with its distracting fish and lumbering alligators, a truly steadfast poet might deny death its proleptic detraction from their writing life, however long it can last.

*

David Ferry's last book, *Some Things I Said*, has the electricity of those existential stakes, and it presents—in a novel way—some measure of what he got "said" as a poet and translator. The book consists of a tightly curated group of 38 poems, including the titular poem, the lines of which relate, as a metaphysical index, to 33 other poems and 4 translations, from different parts of Ferry's oeuvre. Published in a beautiful hardback by the Grolier Series of Established Poets (of the Grolier Poetry Book Shop), *Some Things I Said* proves that Ferry's work was "one long poem" (to borrow from Elizabeth Bishop's assessment of her own work), which reached its apogee in his last decades.

Consider the opening passage of the title poem, which is composed of 39 fragments, alluring in their disjunctive assembly.

> writings on the wall
> *
>
> I was the one who said
> the ditch in the backyard was maybe a river
> that had flowed from somewhere else and was flowing to
> somewhere else
> *
>
> I was the one who said where are you now?
> *

I was the one who told about the one whose photograph in
the book of Eakins's photographs was of
a guy the perfection of his body was his doom, and
Shakespeare said so too
                         *

Right there before my eyes was the one who said
where are you now? Where
are you Anne? I was the one
                         *

Who saw how Aeneas lay there in the darkness watching the
light, the little motions of light moving around the ceiling
and telling him something

                         *

[. . .]

                         *

I said be keep to your self be close be wall all dark

When I first heard Ferry read the poem in 2019, at the College of Holy
Cross in Worcester, I wasn't the only person in the audience transfixed
by this "new" version of his voice. He had broken from the elegance
of blank verse, long part of his signature style, and created a tone vatic
and humane in a poem of astonishing power. As he read, he paused
between fragments with deliberateness but not ostentation, as echoes
redoubled in meaning and the poem built in its cumulative, modernist
force. When he reached the line above, which ends "be close be wall
all dark," I heard these thunderous imperatives against the poem's first
line ("writings on the wall") and an intimation of death in "all dark,"
a relinquishing of one's self to the "wall" of what has been written.
In many ways, this book (and this introductory poem) are this poet's
writings on the wall: what he perhaps most wanted to be read and
remembered.

Repetitions of "I was the one" also lend the poem its annunciatory
pitch, reinforced by a deliberate awkwardness in the syntax, such as the
elocution "I was the one who told about the one," a line that mimics the
confession of a playground tattletale or a barroom braggart. Tones of
age and youth blend here, provocatively. We notice too that the poem
begins with beginnings, as "writings on the wall" are among the ear-
liest testaments of intelligent life: humans trying to express facts about

their existence. Or, *the fact* of their existence. Yet, "writings on the wall" also suggests what children do when first enamored with marking up paper, bedroom walls, their own limbs, and other obliging surfaces.

From this wink at childhood, we segue to a backyard ditch by Ferry's childhood home in which, in the magical realism of youth, he believes there is a river from elsewhere. As the poet describes this early desire to transfigure the landscape, we recall that he wrote *The Limits of Mortality: An Essay on Wordsworth's Major Poems*, one of his two books on Wordsworth, though he was affectionately ironic about Romanticism's enthusiasms later in life. (In the poem "Ancestral Lines," from his collection *Bewilderment*, Ferry quips: "You can't tell anything much about who you are / By exercising on the Romantic bars.") Over the course of his career, he began to think in terms more inspired by Horace and Virgil than by Wordsworth and Keats, Johnson and Pope; in many ways, the classics made Ferry modern, broadening the aperture of what his poems countenance, introducing new subjects to his work. Indeed, locating "who you are" is the major aim in *Some Things I Said*, even if it results in the call—and echo—of a lonesome voice, one the reader can feel in his or her mouth.

In this opening poem, arguably Ferry's *summa*, a poet known for his restraint indulges in headlong parataxis as he grapples with the texture of a long life—its hallway of echoes—and the impress of death, disease, and warfare: the trio of scourges no one escapes for long. He moves from the haunting assertion (and question) "I was the one who said where are you now?" to Eakins's photograph of a perfectly embodied man, one seemingly doomed by his beauty. And from there, we confront the dooms of love in a plaintive repetition of "where are you now?", a query addressed to Ferry's late wife, the accomplished literary scholar Anne Davidson Ferry, the author of seven books, who suffered from Alzheimer's in her later years.

Yet before we can take in this personal tragedy, one of the quickening crises in Ferry's life, the poem shifts to Book VIII of the *Aeneid*, when Aeneas, about to wage war in Latium, feels his worries flit inside of his head like sunlight or moonlight in a bowl of water. In his derangement, the hero believes that the light is "telling" him something as he looks to nature for spiritual sustenance, a thirst that Ferry seems to have suspected could not be quenched. Indeed, at the end of "Some Things

I Said," which approximates the rich layering of time and experience, memory and desire, the speaker of the poem looks again to the light:

What's in the way the sun shines down, I said

*

I cried in my mute heart,
What is my name and nature

The clause "what's in the way" can be read at least two ways: whatever proves to be an obstacle to sunlight is shone "down" as a legible shadow. At the same time, the speaker might also be inquiring about the nature of sunlight, its "way." How are the true identities of things revealed?

What the poet desires most, it seems, is the Orphic power to know and name himself accurately. Cleverly, the conclusion of this poem riffs from two other poems in Ferry's collection including the poem "Garden Dog," which describes a dog exploring a suburban backyard in winter, "sniffing / For enemies burrowed in Ireland // Sometime in the nineteenth century." For all of his deep seriousness, Ferry's wry humor is never far underground. He suggests, in fact, that the desire to "sniff / For enemies" and to know one's "nature" are defining features of us, as creatures. The terrier nuzzling the "dormant / Unflourishing grass in the garden" is akin to the heartsick poet, sitting at a bar, looking into his glass and wishing it were an accurate mirror.

To approximate the shapes of things in the shadows of one's evolving knowledge is at the heart of Ferry's endeavor, although the terms of this quest surfaced quietly, over six decades of writing, as the poet—in his humility—apprenticed himself to the literary tradition as a scholar and translator, finding his voice through other voices.

*

Curious about the arc of Ferry's development, especially the books he published *before* the astonishing ten books published in the last third of his life, I went looking for his first collection, *On the Way to the Island* (1960). The poet was about 35 years-old when it appeared, and the title seems—on the surface—to be a bucolic reference to a New England vacation. A collection of 34 poems, it is lushly neo-Romantic, decorous in its portrayal of marital love, a soldier's service, the New England shore, and suburban wildlife. It is startling to think that this book, a paean to "sober love, in chance and change" that meditates on Adam and Eve, picnics and milkmaids, aging relatives, and the beach at night, appeared virtually alongside Robert Lowell's *Life Studies* (1959), Anne Sexton's *To Bedlam and Part Way Back* (1960), Amiri Baraka's (LeRoi Jones's) *Preface to a Twenty-Volume Suicide Note*, Sylvia Plath's *The Colossus and Other Poems* (1960), and James Wright's *The Branch Will Not Break* (1963), books that radically recast the molds and modes of American poetry. Beside these contemporaries, Ferry must have seemed a lonesome Sibelius, creating pleasing melodies alongside a raucous chorus of atonal Schoenbergs.

On the Way to the Island provides a map for Ferry's early concerns. It includes a translation of Pierre de Ronsard's sonnet that is the basis of W.B. Yeats's poem "When You are Old"; a portrait of Alexander Pope, trussed in his "canvas bodice" in order to stand up; the maturing of "hot ignorant" love into companionate trust; and a soldier refusing a "night pass" from the barracks in order to write a letter to his beloved. I found myself returning to this last poem, "The Soldier," in which the serviceman writes to his inamorata while observing a spider, which "hangs by the thread of its guts." While the poem does not recount the speaker's experience of war, there is another poem, "Learning from History," in which the speaker ridicules the older generation, who sent him and his peers to war with a host of empty platitudes: "They stood, my fathers, tall in a row and said, / Be good, be brave, you shall not come to harm." Indeed, this first book, for all of its mahogany polish and fealty to eighteenth and nineteenth century models, is also an argument with the mass manufactured platitudes of American life, the simplistic stories of heroism in triumphalist America in "which to be / Was to be deaf to the terror sung / In the dream country's charmèd tongue."

While there is nothing in this book that could not be read, aloud, in a 1950s classroom at Wellesley College or at a garden party in metro-Boston, the reader can detect the poet's desire to say more and push further, propelled perhaps by what Wallace Stevens would call "a new knowledge of reality." When the book appeared, the poet-professor had already entered early middle age, duly tending his students and colleagues as a long serving department chair and, with his wife Anne, an English professor at Boston College, raising two children to their own professional accomplishment.

Notably, there are five poems in this first book that reappear, some in altered form or title, in the poet's last book, published sixty-four years later. This suggests that Ferry saw a through-line between his debut and his final collection, and they plot the early emergence of his major themes. These poems—"A Farewell," "On the Way to the Island," "Musings of Mind and Body," "At a Low Bar," and "For the Birthday of Miss Marianne Moore, Whenever Her Birthday Is"—are DNA strands of Ferry's development, a braid of somewhat darker poems (without milkmaids or the Biblical Adam) in which we hear the "sober" lover and scholar, resistant to blandishments, who knew that death would one day bring a seemingly charmed life to its absolute conclusion and include, as well, "fish, huge, munching, graceless, flashing / … [with] frightening scales in the dark." The boat ride to the island would, in fact, come to an end, and Ferry—at 35 years of age—anticipates some of the primordial sea creatures who would appear to test both courage and will.

*

In his poem, "A Farewell," which appears in his first book and in his last, Ferry writes: "Knowledge began with the pressure of light on the eye / And the ear spun out of thin air its airy tune," lines that suggest that, as Horace argued, the poet was born, not made. Yet looking at Ferry's final book draws this Horatian adage into question. Ferry seems to have been both born *and* made a poet, in a rare combination of talent and lifelong labor. When he "retired" from Wellesley College in 1989, where he had taught courses in his wheelhouse (Romantic and twentieth-century poetry, eighteenth-century literature, Shakespeare, and the novel), he taught himself Latin and essentially embarked on a second career as one of the most admired and praised translators of classical literature: a hardy conduit for other voices as he enlivened the Sumerian *Epic of Gilgamesh*, the major poems of Horace, and Virgil's *Aeneid*—all with contemporary verve.

This classical training, obtained later in life, was also a kind of post-modern exercise, an opening of new valves in his own voice. In *Some Things I Said*, Ferry includes a translation of Horace's famous "carpe diem" ode, a phrase that is mistranslated by gym teachers, travel companies, and tee-shirts everywhere as "seize the day" in a militarizing of the agricultural verb *carpo,* which means to pluck, gather, or harvest. Ferry's translation evokes the tender warning in the poem's erotic entreaty: it is better to harvest the day's available pleasure instead of fretting about what only the fates control.

> Don't be too eager to ask
> > What the gods have in mind for us,
> What will become of you,
> > What will become of me,
> What you can read in the cards,
> > Or spell out on the Ouija board.
> [...]
> The time we have is short.
> > Cut short your hopes for longer.
> Now as I say these words,
> > Time has already fled
> Backwards away—
> > Leuconoë—
> > > Hold on to the day.

Horace's ode, which inaugurated the "carpe diem" mode in lyric poetry, is one in which the speaker urges his beloved to desist from her "Babylonian numbers" (or horoscope readings) and instead to "pluck" or "hold" the day. In the Latin, the sensual context is palpable, and in Ferry's translation, the horror that awaits us all—the tide of loss, the finality of mortality itself—isn't worth prognostication. Instead, he urges—in the voice of Horace—"Be mindful. / Take good care of your household. / … Cut short your hopes for longer." As longevity gurus induce us to increase our health spans, using biometrics to surpass the forecasts of actuarial charts, Ferry's brilliant personification of Time itself as a fleeing lover tempers the cultural fever to actualize our physiques. And he rebuts the positivity police who would deny the legitimate seasoning of sadness.

Ferry's translation of Horace's ode, which feels stunningly "new" in his articulation, suggests how his classical training also prepared him to detail—with candor and incisiveness—the hinterlands of one's 80s and 90s, the frontiers of age that the Boomers will explore in ever greater numbers: a demesne, in previous generations, to which few ventured and from which few could report. In this arena of human life, Ferry is bringing us the news: and while it is not entirely sanguine, his humor and compassionate insight are at the fore as he relates what it means to lose a beloved and what it is like to occupy an elderly body. In the poem "That Now Are Wild and Do Not Remember," Ferry seems to allude to his experience of losing his wife, who had been his intellectual companion in a Shakespearean marriage of "true minds." We hear, too, allusions to Sir Thomas Wyatt's "They Flee from Me" in both the poem's title and in these lines:

> Where did you go to, when you went away?
> It is as if you step by step were going
> Someplace elsewhere into some other range
> Of speaking, that I had no gift for speaking,
> Knowing nothing of the language of that place
> To which you went with naked foot at night
> Into the wilderness there elsewhere in the bed,
> Elsewhere somewhere in the house beyond my seeking.

The poet conveys the acute bewilderment of caring for someone who has gone "away," exiting his or her mind to a "wilderness there elsewhere in the bed" or in the house, "beyond my seeking." In the poem, the speaker reports feeling "so dislanguaged" by the loss of his beloved interlocutor that he can hardly find words to describe it. The Eurydice-like circumstance of dementia or Alzheimer's in which a person's mind, personality, and memory disappear—though also, in moments of lucidity, reappear briefly—is captured poignantly by Ferry's Orpheus-like speaker, fated to watch his wife's vanishing not for a tragic moment, but for anguishing years.

In one of the book's most striking poems, "The White Skunk," Ferry's narrator recounts watching an albino skunk, in a redux of Robert Lowell's "Skunk Hour," chase a neighbor and his daughter across a lawn. Observing the skunk, a "near-sighted / Creature [that] read[s] the ground for information," the speaker thinks of someone, presumably Anne Ferry, trapped inside of a memory care unit.

> The walls of the facility at Mount Auburn
> Where she kept wandering the halls, reading blank walls
> To see if there was an exit there, or maybe
> A bulletin board telling her what to do,
> Telling her how to be there, or where to be,

Or what she was trying to find, or where she was going,
Intently studying where it was she was.

The skunk's study of the ground morphs into the woman's desperate effort to interpret her surroundings, searching for an exit or instruction. Here, the "blank walls" of the institution recall the "writings on the wall" in the first line of the book, and this echo heightens the pathos: for a decorated literary scholar to be, at the end of her life, without a reliable mind, memory, or language is a tragedy at once commonplace in our century, as scores of people outlive their minds, and a fall from grace so precipitous, unyielding, and unfair as to counter any notion of such suffering being part of a divine plan.

Facing such extreme loss might have been a greater storm for Ferry to weather than his service in the United States Army Air Force in the 1940s or his nearly four decades of distinguished teaching at a selective college or the prodigious challenge of translating Virgil's 9,883-line *Aeneid*, which he completed at the age of 93. Ferry's gift is finding "symbols adequate to our predicament," to borrow again from Heaney's phrasing, drawing on a profound knowledge of the Western literary tradition that likely rivaled most other poets born in the 1920s. In his late work, we sense the balanced weight of such knowledge and seasoned experience brought to the page. His gentlemanliness, warmth, and superb good manners are always in his work—even when he must tell difficult truths. If *Some Things I Said* is a haunting remix of his life's work, it is also another model of poetic development. Consider these lines from his poem "Soul," in which the psyche reckons with its bodily shell, using a particularly New England, which is to say crustacean, cast of metaphor:

What am I doing inside this old man's body?
I feel like I'm the insides of a lobster,
All thought, and all digestion, and pornographic
Inquiry, and getting about, and bewilderment,
And fear, avoidance of trouble, belief in what,
God knows, vague memories of friends, and what
They said last night, and seeing, outside of myself,
From here inside myself, my waving claws . . .

We can't help but hear the tacit allusion to Eliot's lines, "I should have been a pair of ragged claws / Scuttling across the floors of silent seas" in "The Love Song of Alfred J. Prufrock," a poem in which an early middle-aged narrator expresses anxiety about the waning appeal of his diminished body, his thinning limbs and dwindling hair. In Ferry's poem, the soul negotiates the noise of the geriatric interior, "All thought, and all digestion, and pornographic / Inquiry" without the super-structure of religious belief or the solace of an intimate partner as he calculates "getting about," while managing "fear" and "bewilderment." The ways in which physical frailty might give the soul new direction, if not stern challenge, is brought home in this lyric, whatever the reader's age.

And Ferry's audience of readers grew with each decade. His stature as a poet was amplified by his winning of the National Book Award for his collection *Bewilderment* (2012) when he was 86. In conversation, he would jest that the award felt "posthumous," and when we were reading together at a poetry festival, some ten years ago, he joked that he was "so old, it's obscene!" But his example of growing as an artist, over sixty-odd years of work, was (and is) a heartening rebuttal to the ideal of the *enfant terrible*, who is expected to emerge, fully formed, in their mid-twenties, armed with twelve manuscripts in four genres and a Ph.D. in creative writing.

A night cereus of fierce "late" bloom, Ferry was not, in this era of technocracy and meme-driven writing, checking his online sales or fertilizing his feed of digital disciples. He was speaking to us, as well as to those Muriel Rukeyser called the "unborn and unseen," in colloquy with the ancients and his contemporaries while angling for the ear of a sempiternal listener. He left "writings on the wall" that will likely outlast many of his peers' efforts, in the long sort that posterity makes of writers, as he joins the ranks of the great poets he most admired.

Contributor Notes

LAUREN K. ALLEYNE serves as executive director of the Furious Flower
Poetry Center and professor of English at James Madison University. She
is author of two collections, *Honeyfish* (2019) and *Difficult Fruit* (2014), and
co-editor of *Furious Flower: Seeding the Future of African American Poetry*. Her work
appears in *The Atlantic*, *The New York Times*, and *Ms.*, and has received an
NAACP Image Award nomination for Outstanding Poetry (2020).

FRANCISCO ARAGÓN, a native of San Francisco, California, is the son
of Nicaraguan immigrants. His books include *After Rubén* (2020), *Glow of Our
Sweat* (2010), and *Puerta de Sol* (2005). He directs Letras Latinas, the literary
initiative at the University of Notre Dame's Institute for Latino Studies. For
more information, visit: http://franciscoaragon.net

DAVID BLAIR teaches poetry in the MFA Writing Program at the University
of New Hampshire and lives with his family in Somerville, Massachusetts. His
recent books of poetry include *Barbarian Seasons* and *True Figures: Selected Shorter
Poems and Prose Poems, 1998-2021*.

ANN-MARIE BROWN is a contemporary Canadian artist, painting in oil
and encaustic (wax). She has lived and worked in studios around the globe, and
is currently painting on the west coast of British Columbia in the company of
rain and bears.

MARY BUCHINGER, whose recent collections include *The Book of Shores* and
Virology (Lily Poetry Review Books), and *Navigating the Reach* (Salmon Poetry,
longlisted for the Massachusetts Book Award), teaches at the Massachusetts
College of Pharmacy and Health Sciences. Her poetry appears in *AGNI*,
Nimrod, *Plume*, *Salamander*, *Salt Hill*, *Seneca Review*, and elsewhere. Visit: www.
MaryBuchinger.com

TINA CANE is the founder/director of Writers-in-the-Schools, Rhode Island,
and, from 2016-2024, served as the Poet Laureate of Rhode Island. Cane is
the author of *The Fifth Thought, Dear Elena: Letters for Elena Ferrante, Once More
With Feeling* (Veliz Books, 2017), and *Body of Work* (Veliz Books, 2019). She was
a 2020 Poet Laureate Fellow with the Academy of American Poets and the
creator/curator of the distance reading series, Poetry is Bread. Her most recent
poetry collection is *Year of the Murder Hornet* (Veliz Books, 2022), and her debut
novel-in-verse for young adults, *Alma Presses Play* (Penguin/Random House)
was released in September 2021. Her second novel-in-verse for young readers,
Are You Nobody Too? (Penguin/ Random House) was published in summer 2024.

EILEEN CLEARY (she/her/hers) is the author of *Child Ward of the
Commonwealth* (2019), *2 a.m. with Keats*, and *Wild Pack of the Living*. She founded
and is editor-in-chief of Lily Poetry Review Books and *Lily Poetry Review*. A
multiple-Pushcart Prize nominee, her work is widely published in journals

and anthologies.

ELLE CHU is a Boston-based poet with a BFA from Emerson College. She was a 2019 recipient of the Leonard A. Slade Jr. Fellowship from Martha's Vineyard Institute of Creative Writing and 2023 recipient of the Fine Arts Work Center Scholarship from the city of Boston. Her work appears in *The Fjords Review, The Kindling Collective, Fearsome Critters: The Laurel Review,* and *CAGIBI.* She serves as associate poetry editor for *Consequence Forum.*

ANDREA COHEN is the author of eight books of poetry, including, most recently, *The Sorrow Apartments.* Her poems have appeared in *The New Yorker, The Threepenny Review, The New York Review of Books* and elsewhere. She directs the Blacksmith House Poetry Series in Cambridge, Massachusetts.

MARTHA COLLINS'S eleventh book of poetry is *Casualty Reports* (Pittsburgh, 2022); her tenth, *Because What Else Could I Do* (Pittsburgh, 2019), won the William Carlos Williams Award. Her fifth volume of co-translated Vietnamese poetry is *Dreaming the Mountain* by Tuệ Sỹ (Milkweed, 2023). Her website is marthacollinspoet.com

PATRICK COTTER lives and writes in Cork, Ireland. *Quality Control at the Miracle Factory,* his fourth collection, is coming from Dedalus Press, Dublin, in 2025. His poems appear in the *Financial Times,* the *London Review of Books, POETRY* and *Poetry Review,* among other journals, and have been translated into over a dozen languages. Recipient of the Keats-Shelly Prize, he has read throughout the northern hemisphere.

BRAD CRENSHAW has published four collections of poetry. His most recent book, *Chased by Lunacies and Wonders,* won the 2023 Catamaran Poetry Prize. His other books include *My Gargantuan Desire, Genealogies,* and *Memphis Shoals,* and his work has appeared in a range of journals and anthologies. Visit: https://bradcrenshaw.me/

TOM DALEY'S poetry has been published in *Witness, North American Review, Poetry Ireland Review, Fence, Massachusetts Review* and elsewhere. *House You Cannot Reach—Poems in the Voice of My Mother and Other Poems* and *Far Cry* are his poetry collections. He leads workshops in poetry and memoir writing.

HOWIE FAERSTEIN'S collection, *STAY* (Human Error Publishing), was published in February 2023. His poetry and reviews appear in *Nimrod, Rattle, Cutthroat, Nine Mile, Verse Daily, Nixes Mate, On the Seawall,* and *Connotation.* He also facilitates a weekly poetry discussion group through the Forbes Library in Northampton, Massachusetts. A Pushcart nominee, Cutthroat Discovery Poet, and recipient of the NOVA 2022 poetry prize, he lives in Florence, Massachusetts. Visit: https://howiefaerstein.com

JENNIFER FRANKLIN is the author of three books including *If Some God Shakes Your House* (Four Way Books, 2023), finalist for the 2024 Paterson Poetry Prize and the 2023 Julie Suk Award. Franklin has received a Pushcart Prize, a NYFA/City Artist Corps grant, and a CRCF Award. She is poetry reviews co-editor of *The Rumpus* and teaches at Manhattanville's MFA program, 24 Pearl Street, and HVWC, where she serves as program director.

JOSEPH FRASER is a writer based in Washington, D.C. His poetry also appears in *Berfrois* and *The Arts Fuse*.

APRIL GIBSON is a poet, writer, and professor from the South Side of Chicago. Her work has appeared in *The Kenyon Review, Michigan Quarterly Review, Rhino Poetry, Prairie Schooner,* and elsewhere. Her debut poetry collection *The Span of a Small Forever* was published by Amistad/HarperCollins in 2024.

SARAH GIRAGOSIAN is the author of the collections *Queer Fish*, a winner of the American Poetry Journal Book Prize (Dream Horse Press, 2017), and *The Death Spiral* (Black Lawrence Press, 2020). *Mother Octopus* (Middle Creek Press, 2024) is a co-winner of the Halcyon Prize. Sarah's writing has appeared in *Orion, Ecotone* and *Prairie Schooner,* among other journals.

DEBORAH GORLIN is the author of three collections: *BODILY COURSE,* winner of the White Pine Poetry Press Prize (1997); *LIFE OF THE GARMENT,* winner of the 2014 May Sarton New Hampshire Poetry Prize; and *OPEN FIRE* (Bauhan, 2023). Emerita co-director of the Writing Program at Hampshire College, she served for many years as a poetry editor at *The Massachusetts Review.*

MATTHEW GREENFIELD co-manages Rethink Education, a venture capital firm focused on unlocking the potential of people from marginalized groups. His poems appear in *Raritan, Paris Review, Tikkun,* and *Western Humanities Review,* and he has taught at Bowdoin College, CUNY, and Columbia University.

MYRONN HARDY is the author of, most recently, *Aurora Americana* (Princeton University Press, 2023). His poems have appeared in the *New York Times Magazine, Ploughshares, POETRY,* the *Georgia Review, The Baffler,* and elsewhere. He lives in Maine.

CHARLES O. HARTMAN has published eight collections of poetry including *Downfall of the Straight Line* (Arrowsmith Press, 2024), as well as books on jazz and song (*Jazz Text,* Princeton 1991) and on computer poetry (*Virtual Muse,* Wesleyan 1996). His *Verse: An Introduction to Prosody* was published by Wiley-Blackwell in 2015. He is Poet in Residence Emeritus at Connecticut College.

MATTHEW E. HENRY (MEH) is an educator, prose dabbler, and the author of six poetry collections. He is editor-in-chief of *The Weight Journal* and an associate editor at *Rise Up Review*. MEH can be found at www. MEHPoeting.com writing about education, race, religion, and burning oppressive systems to the ground.

RICHARD HOFFMAN is the author of many books, including the Massachusetts Book Award winning *Noon until Night*, and the recent *People Once Real*. He is Emeritus writer-in-residence at Emerson College and nonfiction editor of *Solstice: A Magazine of Diverse Voices*.

ELAINE JOHANSON is a Philadelphia based writer and artist. In 2020, she published *AND AND* (Elm Twig Press), a chapbook of poems and photographs with photographer Jan C. Almquist that explores her family's history and her Korean identity.

CHRISTINE JONES is the author of *Now Calls Me Daughter* (Nixes Mate Review, 2022) and *Girl Without a Shirt* (Finishing Line Press, 2020); co-editor of the anthology, *Voices Amidst the Virus: Poets Respond to the Pandemic* (Lily Poetry Books, 2020); associate editor of *Lily Poetry Review*; and co-founder of the Lily on the Cove Manuscript Clinic and Retreat.

KIRUN KAPUR is a poet, editor, teacher and translator. She is the author of three books of poetry, *Visiting Indira Gandhi's Palmist* (Elixir Press, 2015), which won the Arts & Letters Rumi Prize and the Antivenom Poetry Award; *Women in the Waiting Room* (Black Lawrence Press, 2020), a finalist for the National Poetry Series; and the chapbook *All the Rivers in Paradise* (UChicago Arts, 2022). Her work appears in *AGNI*, *Poetry International*, *Prairie Schooner*, and *Ploughshares*. She serves as editor at the *Beloit Poetry Journal* and teaches at Amherst College, where she is director of the Creative Writing Program.

ALI KINSELLA'S co-translation with Dzvinia Orlowsky from the Ukrainian of Natalka Bilotserkivets's poems, *Eccentric Days of Hope and Sorrow* (Lost Horse Press, 2021) was a finalist for the 2022 Griffin Poetry Prize. They were awarded an NEA fellowship for their recent volume of Halyna Kruk's poetry in translation, *Lost in Living* (Lost Horse Press, 2024). She won the 2019 Kovaliv Fund Prize for her translation of Taras Prokhasko's *Anna's Other Days* and a 2021 Peterson Literary Fund grant to translate Vasyl Makhno's *Eternal Calendar*. She co-edited *Love in Defiance of Pain: Ukrainian Stories* (Deep Vellum Publishing, 2022), an anthology of short fiction to support Ukrainians during the war.

ALYSE KNORR is an associate professor of English at Regis University and co-editor of Switchback Books. She is the author of the poetry collections *Ardor* (2023), a Lambda Literary Award finalist, as well as *Mega-City Redux* (2017), *Copper Mother* (2016), and *Annotated Glass* (2013).

VIRGINIA KONCHAN is the author of five books of poetry, *Requiem* (Carnegie Mellon University Press, 2025); *Bel Canto* (Carnegie Mellon, 2022); *Hallelujah Time* (Véhicule Press, 2021); *Any God Will Do* and *The End of Spectacle* (Carnegie Mellon, 2010 and 2018), and a short story collection, *Anatomical Gift*. She co-edited *Marbles on the Floor: How to Assemble a Book of Poems* (University of Akron Press, 2023) and has received fellowships from the Amy Clampitt Poet

Residency Program and the National Endowment for the Humanities; her poems appear in *The New Yorker*, *The New Republic*, *The Atlantic*, *The Believer*, and the *Academy of American Poets*.

HALYNA KRUK is an award-winning author of five books of poetry in addition to her prose. Her translators for *Lost in Living* (Lost Horse Press, 2024) were awarded a NEA grant and her previous book, *A Crash Course in Molotov Cocktails*, was a 2024 Griffin Prize finalist. She lives and works in Lviv, Ukraine.

JUNE DAOWEN LEI is an art worker, poet, and a lifelong New Yorker. She is currently a master's student in Labor Studies at the City University of New York. She was a Kundiman Mentorship Fellow in 2019. Her writing has been published in the *Brooklyn Rail*, *Columbia Journal*, and Poets.org.

SARAH LEIDHOLD enjoys writing, reading, dancing, exploring nature, and connecting with others. She lives in Massachusetts with her partner, their dog, and an array of anthropomorphized house plants.

NINA MACLAUGHLIN is the author of *Wake, Siren* (FSG), a finalist for the Lambda Literary Award and the Massachusetts Book Award, as well as *Summer Solstice* and *Winter Solstice* (Black Sparrow), winner of the 2024 Massachusetts Book Award in nonfiction. Her first book was the acclaimed memoir *Hammer Head: The Making of a Carpenter* (W.W. Norton), a finalist for the New England Book Award. Formerly an editor at the *Boston Phoenix*, she worked for nine years as a carpenter, and is now a books columnist for the *Boston Globe*. She lives in Cambridge, Massachusetts.

JENNIFER MARTELLI is the author of *The Queen of Queens*, winner of the Italian American Studies Association Book Award, and *My Tarantella*, named a "Must Read" by the Massachusetts Center for the Book. Martelli has been awarded fellowships from The Massachusetts Cultural Council and the VCCA.

ALEX MAYER is a writer based in Philadelphia, Pennsylvania. She earned her MFA in Creative Writing from the University of South Carolina, and her writing appears in *On the Seawall*, *Harvard Review*, and *Green Mountains Review*.

PATTIE MCCARTHY is the author of seven books of poetry, most recently *Wifthing* (Apogee Press, 2021), and a dozen chapbooks, most recently *extraordinary tides* (Omnidawn Publishing, 2023) and *three tides* (Bloof Books 2022). A former Pew Fellow in the Arts, she is a non-tenure track professor at Temple University where she teaches literature and creative writing.

MARTHA MCCOLLOUGH'S forthcoming book is *Trash Witch* (2025). She is the author of *Wolf Hat Iron Shoes* (2022) and the chapbook *Grandmother Mountain* (Blue Lyra, 2019). Her poems appear in *Pleiades*, *The Boiler*, *Radar Poetry*, and *Bear Review*, among other journals. Originally from Detroit, she lives in

Amherst, Massachusetts.

ORLANDO RICARDO MENES, professor of English at the University of
Notre Dame, is the author of seven poetry collections, including *The Gospel
of Wildflowers & Weeds* (University of New Mexico Press, 2022), *and Fetish*
(University of Nebraska Press, 2013), winner of the 2012 Prairie Schooner
Book Prize in Poetry.

SUZANNE MERCURY is the author of *Hive* (Lily Poetry Review Books) as
well as two chapbooks, *Sassafracas* (2018, Xexoxial Editions), and *Hand to Earth*
(2019, Portable Press at Yo-Yo Labs). Her work appears in a variety of publica-
tions and anthologies. She lives in Boston where she also keeps bees.

JENNIFER MILITELLO is the Poet Laureate of New Hampshire. She is
the author of the forthcoming hybrid collection *Identifying the Pathogen* (Tupelo
Press, 2025); the memoir *Knock Wood*, winner of the Dzanc Nonfiction Prize;
and five collections of poetry, including, most recently, *The Pact* (Tupelo Press/
Shearsman Books, 2021). Her work appears in *Best American Poetry, Best New
Poets, American Poetry Review, The Nation, The New Republic, The Paris Review, and
Poetry*. She teaches in the MFA program at New England College.

ELLEN MILLER-MACK is a poet, nurse practitioner, and blues lover. She
has an MFA in Poetry from Drew University, and her poetry book reviews can
be found online. "Hot Tamale Blues" can be heard weekly at WMUA 91.1
FM, www.wmua.org. She also co-hosts "Poet Talk," also on WMUA, which is
archived at poemtalk.transistor.fm.

ASKOLD MELNYCZUK has published four novels, which have been
variously named a *New York Times* Notable Book, an *LA Times* Best Book of
the Year, and an Editor's Choice by *Booklist*. He is also the author of a book of
stories, *The Man Who Would Not Bow*, and editor of a book on Derek Walcott as
well as an anthology of contemporary Ukrainian poetry and fiction. Founding
editor of *Agni*, he is the publisher of Arrowsmith Press and recipient of the
George Garret Award from AWP for his contributions to the literary commu-
nity.

GLORIA MONAGHAN is professor of humanities at Wentworth University.
She has published six collections of poetry. Her most recent, *Cormorant on the
Strand,* was published by Lily Poetry Review (2023). Her poems appear in
Alexandria Quarterly, NPR, Poem-a-Day, Lily Poetry Review, and *Mom Egg Review,*
among other venues.

AYAZ MURATOGLU is a poet, essayist, and translator living in Brooklyn,
New York. Their work has appeared or is forthcoming in *The Poetry Project
Newsletter, Yalobusha Review, Landfill, The Critical Flame, pan-pan press*, and *On the
Seawall*. Ayaz was born on a Tuesday in April in Boston, Massachusetts.

JEFFERSON NAVICKY is the author of four books, most recently *Head of
Island Beautification for the Rural Outlands* (2023) as well as *Antique Densities: Modern*

Parables & Other Experiments on Short Prose (2021), which won the 2022 Maine Literary Award for Poetry. He works as the archivist for the Maine Women Writers Collection and lives in rural midcoast Maine.

DZVINIA ORLOWSKY'S co-translations with Ali Kinsella include Natalka Bilotserkivets's *Eccentric Days of Hope & Sorrow*, a 2022 Griffin Poetry Prize finalist and 2022 AAUS Translation Prize winner, and Halyna Kruk's *Lost in Living*, for which they received a 2024 NEA Translation Fellowship. Orlowsky's newest poetry collection, *Those Absences Now Closest*, is forthcoming in 2024.

KATHLEEN OSSIP'S books of poetry include *July*, one of NPR's best books of 2021. She teaches at The New School and at Princeton University, and she has been a fellow at Harvard University's Radcliffe Institute.

KATE PARTRIDGE is the author of two poetry collections: *THINE* (Tupelo, 2023) and *Ends of the Earth* (University of Alaska, 2017). Her poems appear in *FIELD, Yale Review, Pleiades, Michigan Quarterly Review, Copper Nickel*, and other journals. She is an assistant professor of English at Regis University in Denver.

TZYNYA PINCHBACK writes of the Black woman's body in nature, illness, and joy. Her chapbook *How to make pink confetti* was selected for the Dancing Girl Press reading series for women poets, and she was a finalist for 2020 Plymouth poet laureate. Pinchback is a 2024 PEN America emerging voices fellow.

ANNE ELEZABETH PLUTO grew up in Brooklyn, New York, before it was cool. She is professor of literature and theatre at Lesley University in Cambridge, Massachusetts, where she is the artistic director of the Oxford Street Players. Her most recent book is *How Many Miles to Babylon?* (Lily Poetry Review Books, 2024).

ELIZABETH A.I. POWELL'S *The Republic of Self* was a New Issue First Book Prize winner, selected by C.K. Williams. Her second book, *Willy Loman's Reckless Daughter* won the Anhinga Robert Dana Prize and was a "Books We Love/ 2016" in *The New Yorker*. Her third book of poems *Atomizer* (LSU Press) appeared in 2020. Her novel *Concerning the Holy Ghost's Interpretation of JCREW Catalogues* was released in the U.K. in 2020. Her work appears in *The New Republic, American Poetry Review*, the *Pushcart Prize Anthology, Women's Review of Books, Ploughshares* and elsewhere. She is professor of creative writing at Vermont State University.

DANIEL E. PRITCHARD is a poet, translator, essayist, and founding editor of *The Critical Flame* (criticalflame.org). Daniel's poems have appeared recently in *The Arts Fuse, Holy Gossip, Pangyrus*, and elsewhere. His debut manuscript was short-listed for the Cardinal Poetry Prize in 2024, and he lives in Greater Boston.

JOSÉ EDMUNDO OCAMPO REYES was born and raised in the Philippines. His collection *Present Values* won the Jean Pedrick Chapbook Prize from the New England Poetry Club. He is a recipient of the Robert H. Winner Memorial Award from the Poetry Society of America.

VIDYAN RAVINTHIRAN teaches at Harvard. His last book of poems, *The Million-Petalled Flower of Being Here*, won a Northern Writers' Award, was a Poetry Book Society Recommendation, and was shortlisted for both the T.S. Eliot and Forward Prizes. His next, *Avidya*, is out in 2025.

DYLAN RICHMOND is a recent Bowdoin College graduate with degrees in dance and English. As a poet, dancer, choreographer, and Mellon Mays Fellow, his interests lie in Ntozake Shange's choreopoem and questions of violence, surveillance, and joy. Dylan calls Madison, Connecticut, his home as well as anywhere there is an ocean.

AMY RODRIGUEZ is an artist living in the Ozark Mountains. Her ongoing project *Asemic Poetica* consists of more than 450 paintings as of 2024. Amy's chapbook of art and poetry, *Light Pours In,* will be available from Anhinga Press this summer.

ANNA V. Q. ROSS'S most recent book, *Flutter, Kick,* won the Benjamin Saltman Poetry Award from Red Hen Press, the Julia Ward Howe Award in Poetry, and was named a 2023 Best New Poetry Book by the New York Public Library. A recipient of grants and fellowships from the Fulbright Foundation and the Massachusetts Cultural Council, her work appears in *Harvard Review, The Kenyon Review,* and *The Nation.*

ELLA SCHMIDT is a poet, fiction writer, and essayist from St. Louis, Missouri. Her work has appeared in *Hobart, Oakland Arts Review, Maudlin House,* and the *Notre Dame Review.* She lives in Boston.

LLOYD SCHWARTZ is the poet laureate of Somerville, Massachusetts, an editor of Elizabeth Bishop, and an arts critic for NPR's *Fresh Air* and WBUR. His awards include fellowships in poetry from the NEA, the Guggenheim Foundation, and the Academy of American Poets, and a Pulitzer Prize for Criticism. His latest book is *Who's on First?: New And Selected Poems.*

J.D. SCRIMGEOUR is the author of five poetry collections, most recently the bilingual 香蕉面包 /Banana Bread (Nixes Mate Press). He won the Association of Writers and Writing Program's (AWP) Award for Nonfiction for *Themes for English B: A Professor's Education In & Out of Class.*

RON SLATE'S new book of poems is *Joy Ride* (Carnegie Mellon University Press). He is the editor and host of the online literary gallery *On The Seawall.*

J.J. STARR's poems appear in *The Common, Juked, The Journal,* and *2 River,* among other journals. She earned a MFA from the creative writing program at NYU, where she was a Veterans Writer's Workshop Fellow. She lives in Massachusetts.

LISA J. SULLIVAN holds an MFA in Poetry from the Solstice Low-Residency MFA Program,where she was a Kurt Brown Memorial Fellow. Her work appears in *Sow's Ear Poetry Review, The American Journal of Poetry, The Comstock Review, Puckerbrush Review,* and elsewhere. Lisa is the Art Editor for *Lily Poetry Review* and a Poetry and Art Editor for *Pink Panther Magazine.*

HEATHER TRESELER's *Auguries & Divinations* received the 2024 Shelia Margaret Motton Book Award. Her work appears in *The American Scholar, PN Review, LARB,* and *Boston Review.* Recipient of *Narrative* magazine's annual poetry prize (2023), she is professor of English at Worcester State University and a resident scholar at the Brandeis Women's Studies Research Center.

MOLLY TWOMEY is a poet living in Cork, Ireland. Her debut collection, *Raised Among Vultures,* was published in 2022 by The Gallery Press. It won the Southword Debut Collection Poetry Award and was shortlisted for the Seamus Heaney Poetry Prize for Best First Collection.

PETER URKOWITZ lives in Salem, Massachusetts, where he works in a college library. He was drawn to the local poetry scene as a spectator and began writing his own work. He has published poems in *Meat for Tea: The Valley Review* and in *Oddball Magazine.* He is the author of *Fake Zodiac Signs: An Astro-Illogical Guidebook.*

HILDE VANDENHOUT is an artist and psychotherapist based in Belgium, professions she feels go well together. She loves working with asemic writing and finds that language is a strong therapeutic medium. The process that takes place between viewer and the image is the real answer to "what does it mean?"

ANTHONY WALTON is the author of *The End of Respectability, Notes of a Black American Reckoning with His Life and His Nation* (Godine), *Mississippi: An American Journey* (Knopf), and other books. With Michael Harper, he edited two anthologies of African American poetry. His poems appear in the *New Yorker, 32 Poems,* and other journals, and in the Library of America's anthology, *African American Poetry: 250 Years of Struggle & Song.*

DYLAN WELCH is a high school English teacher in Oakland, Maine. He holds a Masters of Arts in teaching secondary English from Brown University. He recently published a review in *On the Seawall.* He lives in Midcoast Maine, where he enjoys attending Saturday farmers markets with his partner and cooking up a local meal.